D1152607

SCOTTISH WRITERS

Editor
DAVID DAICHES

ACKNOWLEDGEMENT

The Scottish Academic Press acknowledges the financial assistance of the Scottish Arts Council in the publication of this volume.

JOHN DAVIDSON

MARY O'CONNOR

SCOTTISH ACADEMIC PRESS

EDINBURGH

Published by
Scottish Academic Press Ltd.
33 Montgomery Street, Edinburgh EH7 5JX

First Published 1987
SBN 7073 0366 4

ISBN 0-7073-0366-4

Printed in Great Britain by
Bell and Bain Ltd., Glasgow

CONTENTS

LIST OF ABBREVIATIONS

I. JOHN DAVIDSON

References to *The Poems of John Davidson*, ed. Andrew Turnbull (1973), are given throughout by page number only.

MA	*Miss Armstrong's and Other Circumstances* (1896)
MF	*The Man Forbid and Other Essays* (1910)
MM	*God and Mammon. A Trilogy. Mammon and His Message* (1908)
NW	*The North Wall* (1885)
Theatrocrat	*The Theatrocrat: A Tragic Play of Church and Stage* (1904)
TM	*God and Mammon. A Trilogy. The Triumph of Mammon* (1907)

II. OTHER

BL	British Library
GH	*Glasgow Herald*
PUL	Princeton University Library
TLS	*Times Literary Supplement*

INTRODUCTION

The Life

John Davidson was born in Barrhead, Renfrewshire, on 11 April 1857, the fourth child and first son of the Reverend Alexander Davidson, a minister in the newly-formed Evangelical Union Church, and Helen Crockett, the daughter of a schoolteacher and an elder of the church in Elgin. Davidson grew up in a religious family with a father who came to be known in Greenock, where the family moved when John was two, as a patriarch.[1] If there is nothing obvious in the life of Alexander Davidson to warrant the father-figures in Davidson's poetry, from the cold-hearted Calvinist of 'A Ballad in Blank Verse' (1894) to the castrating king in *The Triumph of Mammon* (1907), he might still have appeared formidable to a young son. The father had had his moments of rebellious heroic action: at fifteen he had stood up in the town of Wick and delivered a memorable Temperance speech, and as a young man had broken away from a parent church to join the Evangelical Union. In Greenock he was known for his sermons and his impressive voice. Davidson once said that people would come from other parishes just to hear him give the benediction.[2] Davidson, who loved the theatre and the music halls, his whisky and cigars, and Swinburne's poetry, would have had much to quarrel over with his father. It is true that, at fifteen, Davidson became a member of his father's church,[3] and in many ways he respected his father, but he spent the rest of his life actively fighting Christianity. It may be significant that his two major poems about the relationship between a son and his parents were written respectively after his father's death and his mother's ('A Ballad in

Blank Verse' and 'A Mother and Her Son'). We know
little about Davidson's mother, beyond the report that
she was religious and intelligent, but it may also be
important that Davidson suffered a severe breakdown
after his mother's death in 1896.

It is clear from Davidson's writing the one luxury he
enjoyed as a child and a young man was the natural
surroundings of Greenock on the Firth of Clyde. His
walks out of Greenock he considered the most beautiful
he had ever seen. Through Wordsworthian eyes, and
perhaps through Whistlerian eyes, he was able to move
between the rural and the urban landscapes with equal
wonder:

                    I need
      No world more spacious than the region here:
      The foam-embroidered firth, a purple path
      For argosies that still on pinions speed,
      Or fiery-hearted cleave with iron limbs
      And bows precipitous the pliant sea;
      The sloping shores that fringe the velvet tides
      With heavy buillion and with golden lace
      Of restless pebble woven and fine spun sand;
      The villages that sleep the winter through,
      And, wakening with the spring, keep festival
      All summer and all autumn: this grey town
      That pipes the morning up before the lark
      With shrieking steam, and from a hundred stalks
      Lacquers the sooty sky; where hammers clang
      On iron hulls, and cranes in harbours creak
      Rattle and swing, whole cargoes on their necks;
      Where men sweat gold that others hoard or spend,
      And lurk like vermin in their narrow streets:
      This old grey town, this firth, the further strand
      Spangled with hamlets, and the wooded steeps,
      Whose rocky tops behind each other press,
      Fantastically carved like antique helms
      High-hung in heaven's cloudy armoury,
      Is world enough for me. (293)

At the same time that he could see its beauty, he could not deny the poverty and squalor of the industrial shipping port that surrounded him. The Davidsons lived on the edge of the poorer part of Greenock near the Evangelical Union Church. Greenock at the time was a hard and violent town. With high unemployment, it was renowned for its alcoholism and crime rate. Its population had quadrupled in the nineteenth century, mostly under the pressure of a large immigration from Ireland, the Western Highlands, and the Islands. As Eric Northey has pointed out, the town was split between the wealthy few — the shipping magnates, the exporters, and the owners of the sugar mills — and the many poor — the employed or unemployed workers.[4] Davidson would have witnessed the effects of this poverty and crime not only on the street but also in the classroom, for he taught in more than one Charity school. A sense of economic and social injustice, of the dire plight of the working-class man and his family, haunted him throughout his life. If he did not turn to socialism, as some of his contemporaries did, it was not for lack of observation and sympathy.

Davidson had attended the Highlanders' Academy in Greenock and, after working for a short time in Walker's Sugar factory and the public analyst's office in Greenock, he returned to his school as a pupil teacher. In 1876 he spent a year at Edinburgh University studying classics, but took up a teaching post at Alexander's Endowed School, Glasgow, the year after that. Although he said he found teaching 'hellish drudgery'[5] and 'mental boot-blacking',[6] his short story, 'The Schoolboy's Tragedy',[7] and the testimony of at least one student and one colleague indicate that he was sensitive to children and inspired in his teaching. In an unpublished memoir, a friend and colleague of Davidson's, Rudolf von Liebich, wrote that Davidson never had difficulty holding his students' attention.

'They listened with delight to his illuminating lectures on poetry and seemed to devour his every word, entranced. He was far and away the most popular of all the teachers ...'[8] Liebich went on to describe Davidson's heroic organization of his fellow teachers (who included the poet John Barlas) against their rector at Morrison's Academy in Crieff whose cruelty towards the children was the main issue. 'The Schoolboy's Tragedy', perhaps Davidson's best short story, confirms this account of Davidson's sympathy for children. A teacher torments a student until he finally breaks his spirit. As in the case of many other poems and stories, this one is filled with tenderness and understanding for the young boy or girl who is in touch with desires, fantasies, and ambition, but who is restrained by parents, school or society.

Davidson's 'revolution' at Crief failed, and he and Liebich, consequently unemployed, 'undertook a short self-managed tour of Perth, Stirling, Glasgow and a few smaller places..., giving an entertainment [they] named "Dramatic and Musical Recitals"'.[9] However, this acting career was only a short interlude and Davidson was soon back teaching at various schools until 1890 when he moved to London.

His teaching years were in fact some of the most exciting and productive for his literary career, as he found his way into the young literary circles of Glasgow. He had been, it seems, an intelligent, perhaps precocious child (debating predestination at the age of nine; memorizing books such as *Le Morte d'Arthur*, Shakespeare's sonnets, and Milton's *Comus*; and writing poems and plays from an early age).[10] In Glasgow, he attended University classes, becoming one of 'the most gifted of John Nicoll's students'.[11] As the latter's protégé, he was introduced to Swinburne, who chanted Davidson's poetry and, as the story goes, touched his shoulder and pronounced him 'poet'.[12] Around the same time, Davidson seems to have joined the Glasgow Ballad Club, founded in 1876, which met to read traditional and original ballads and lyric poems. Some of the friends Davidson made at this time remained true and close to him throughout his London years: John Cramb (the author of *England and Germany: Reflections on the Origin and Destiny of Imperial Britain*), W. S. McCormick, William Canton, and others.

Davidson married in 1885 (with Cramb as his witness). He took his duties as husband and father to heart (he had two sons), despite his cries for an independent spirit and unfettered life. We have little information about Davidson's wife, Maggie, although J. Benjamin Townsend, Davidson's biographer, quotes a telling letter from her to Grant Richards after Davidson's disappearance in 1909: 'Of course we had differences of opinions — but we had no two ideas in common — that's how we got on so well'.[13]

By the time Davidson left for London in late 1889, he had already published *Diabolus Amans*, *The North Wall*, *Smith*, *Bruce*, and *Plays*, which included *An Unhistorical Pastoral*, *A Romantic Farce*, and *Scaramouch in Naxos*. He had also written a book of short stories, a collection of poems, and at least one other novel, which would all be published during his first years in London.

A number of Davidson's short stories deal with young, aspiring men and women dreaming of being successful in the centre of the English cultural world, London. Alison Hepburn, in 'Alison Hepburn's Exploits',[14] boards the midnight train from Edinburgh with her manuscript of poems tucked under her arm, arriving in the big city only to find dirt and confusion. The instructive all-night train ride opens her eyes to a reality of gruff and sodden passengers. Illusions are shattered, and she returns home on the next train with a more real sense of her identity and worth, having ventured no further than the Euston Road exit of

King's Cross Station. Despite Alison's final resignation, it is a sensitive story about illusions and reality. Another story ('A Would-Be Londoner')[15] tells of a young raconteur who has achieved his fame in Glasgow but now wants to conquer London society. Through a series of introductions he finally meets with an established London figure, but all his memorized *bon mots* fail him at the crucial moment and his desire to please is displaced by a knowledge of failure. In despair he keeps absolutely silent and achieves, in the end, a power over the rest of London society by haunting the streets and cafés in this magnetic silent state. In 'Miss Armstrong's Circumstances',[16] the heroine's desire to succeed with London music publishers drives her to contact those she takes to be influential people in the London musical world only to discover the drudgery and sense of failure they all 'enjoy' in their exalted station.

The Davidsons first moved not to the centre of London but to the suburb of Hornsey, with Davidson commuting to work in Fleet Street. Like the characters in his eclogues he was a literary reviewer and editor who wrote poetry on the side, contributing to as many as eighteen journals and newspapers. He was the editor of a weekly column in the *Speaker* and at one point became the sub-editor of a small short-lived literary journal called *The Weekly Review*. Despite the new form of drudgery, and Davidson did complain of it as such, he quickly made new friends and contacts through his work, frequenting the Rhymers' Club and then the Bodley Head as one of their poets. With his first volume of poems, *In a Music-Hall* (1891), he was described by W. B. Yeats as a leader in the new wave of London writing;[17] by 1894 his 'Ballad of a Nun' became one of the most talked about, quoted (and parodied) poems from the *Yellow Book*, while his *Ballads and Songs* (1894) were referred to as 'the poems of the hour'.[18] There were nineties evenings of absinthe and near brawls in the Café Royal, and dinners at his clubs, the Hogarth, the Grosvenor, or the Savoy. The apogee of his fame was perhaps the production of *For the Crown*, a translation of François Coppée's *Pour la couronne*, which opened at the Lyceum on 27 February 1896, starring Mrs Patrick Campbell and Forbes Robertson. It had a short success, and Davidson was called a major London poet.

All the while, despite the fame and appearance of a gay life, Davidson was always in need of money and always under pressure to write more. He had been helping to support his mother and sister in Edinburgh when his brother, emotionally unstable and an alcoholic, made an attempt on his mother's life.[19] He had to be placed in Garthneven Asylum, and the mother and sister had to be fully supported for almost a year until his mother's death in September 1896. Davidson then arranged to have his brother start a new life in Australia and had his sister come to live with him for six months. The result of all this strain — emotional, financial, and probably profoundly psychological — was a complete nervous and physical breakdown. He moved out of London and spent the next year and a half on the Sussex coast. During his convalescence there in Shoreham, Davidson turned to philosophy. As he said more lightly in a published article: 'When a Scotsman finds himself at cross purposes with life ... [h]e either sits down and drinks deeply, thoughtfully, systematically, of the amber spirit of his country, or he reads philosophy'.[20] Davidson read philosophy: he read Schopenhauer, and Ernst Haeckle (*The Riddle of the Universe*) and even memorized Nietzsche. The poems and plays Davidson wrote from this time on are imbued with his new philosophical discoveries, first of a cosmic irony that governs all of life with its unresolved antitheses, and then, with the help

of the nebular hypothesis, of a scientific materialism
that eliminates all dualities in the unconscious forces of
matter. The new ideas did not sit well with his former
readers or his critics. His return to London, this time to
the south suburb of Streatham, began a long pathetic
history of attempts to write not only poetry for
publication but also plays for the stage.

His former success with *For the Crown* and another
adaptation, *Children of the King* (the Court Theatre, 13
October 1897), brought Davidson commissions for new
adaptations and translations. In September 1899
Beerbohm Tree, the actor-manager, commissioned an
original play which became *Self's the Man*, but he did
not accept it. In December 1899, Davidson made
arrangements with Charles Frohman to do a version of
Catulle Mendes' *Queen Fiametta*, but nothing seems to
have come of them. In the spring of 1901, Davidson
travelled to Blairlogie, a small village in the Ochils, to
translate and adapt Victor Hugo's *Ruy Blas* for Waller.
After many delays, it was finally produced at the
Lyceum in February 1904, but closed after fourteen
days. Davidson made two other trips to Scotland to
work on adaptations: one, a Lancelot play in
November 1902 for George Alexander, and another, a
translation of *Phèdre* for Mrs. Patrick Campbell. Neither
was produced. In 1902 Davidson also wrote 'Fanny
Legrand. A Play in Four Acts adapted from Alphonse
Daudet's Novel "Sappho"', and a copy remains in the
Lord Chamberlain's archives in the British Library, but
it too was not produced. *Bohémos*, also in the British
Library, a one-act comedy adapted by Davidson from
the French of Miguel Zamaçois, was produced at the
Court Theatre on 9 January 1904 with Charles Lauder,
but the critics were not enthusiastic, finding it lacked
the bite and airy lightness of the French *jeu d'esprit*.[21]
Two other original plays, *Godfrida* and *The Knight of the
Maypole*, were published but not produced.

By this time Davidson had changed publishers and was embarked on a series of 'Testaments' and 'Tragedies' conveying his materialist beliefs. *The Theatrocrat: A Tragic Play of Church and Stage* (1905) might well be described, as Townsend has done, as a 'swan song' to the London stage. The play is set in contemporary London, where an actor-manager of the old school is trying to save his theatre from a takeover by the new American wave of commercial entertainment. He is helped by the Bishop of St. James, who wants to write a great drama of atheistic materialism. The Bishop's prologue enrages the audience so much that they attack and murder the Bishop and destroy the stage set. His play is never begun. Davidson's last act is somewhere between Genêt and Jacobean tragedy, where the only resolution is rage, violence, and martyrdom. Still Davidson had hopes for a critical success, and the book's failure brought him near despair.

It was at this time that Bernard Shaw, interested in Davidson's materialist ideas, offered him £250 to write an original drama. Again Davidson's hopes were raised, and his letters to Shaw reveal the great enthusiasm and energy he had for the project: 'I come out of your shower-bath glowing and refreshed, and can think of nothing but your challenge which I seize with both hands. I will go at once and write such a play as you commission without arière pensee [*sic*] on these capital terms'.[22] Within a week Davidson had left for the quiet and seclusion of St Ives and within two weeks he had 'made a scenario' and begun the first act. Unfortunately the messages were crossed, and Davidson fell into the old trap of trying to write a commercial success. The compromise evidently led to an impossible Shavian prose comedy, although we do not have the play to confirm Shaw's assessment. The misunderstanding was not entirely on Davidson's side; it is clear that Shaw

misled Davidson in the specifications,[23] but Shaw's
unfavourable response to 'The Game of Life', as the
play was called, must have only confirmed Davidson's
earlier decision to retreat from the literary battleground.

He was able to retreat into one entertaining role
which he still felt he could honestly and successfully
fulfill. His prose-writing Random Itinerant once again
was sent journeying, this time through the South-
western counties, writing travel sketches for newspapers.
The walking and the sightseeing lifted his spirits, and
the end result was a rented house in Penzance where he
thought he would spend his winters. By June 1907 he
and his family had moved, ostensibly for health and
financial reasons, but the move was also a final break
with London society. He felt as if he were in exile;
nevertheless, the break produced some powerful poetry:
his *Testament of John Davidson*, the two plays of his
Trilogy, *God and Mammon*, and his last volume, *Fleet
Street and Other Poems*.

His health did not improve: the asthma and
bronchitis were not relieved, and in the end he believed
he had cancer. In February, August, and November
1908 there were signs of severe depression as there must
have been again in March 1909. By August he had
made his will and by the following March, before he
had to face his fifty-second birthday, he disappeared.
Three months later his body was found at sea. The
coroner's verdict was 'accidental death', but the
prefatory note ('The time has come to make an end
...') left with his last manuscript has been generally
accepted as a suicide note.[24] He was buried at sea,
according to his wishes, off Land's End.

Suicide and death had long been a subject of his
poems and plays, but a year before his death he
published his own death song as an accompaniment to
his personal testament, *The Testament of John Davidson*.
'The Last Journey' presents a man ready to die, having
walked the long distance of an overfull life:

I felt the world a-spinning on its nave,
   I felt it sheering blindly round the sun;
I felt the time had come to find a grave:
   I knew it in my heart my days were done.
I took my staff in hand; I took the road,
And wandered out to seek my last abode.
     Hearts of gold and hearts of lead
       Sing it yet in sun and rain,
    'Heel and toe from dawn to dusk,
      Round the world and home again'.

. . . .

Farewell the hope that mocked, farewell despair
   That went before me still and made the pace.
The earth is full of graves, and mine was there
   Before my life began, my resting-place;
And I shall find it out and with the dead
Lie down for ever, all my sayings said —
     Deeds all done and songs all sung,
       While others chant in sun and rain,
    'Heel to toe from dawn to dusk,
      Round the world and home again'. (426–7)

The Works

In a general assessment of John Davidson's work,
Howard Mumford Jones called the poet 'a bitter and
defeated rebel ... who strove vainly all his life against
the limits of Form. Art itself was inadequate for him,
and he desired some new mode of expression into which
he could pour all the "over-stimulating amount of
mental activity" that was in him. Every weapon —
ballad, testament, novel, play — snapped like wood in
his hands'.[25] For a poet who was reputed to place little
emphasis on formal criteria in art, Davidson
consistently called attention to the forms he employed
by naming them in his titles: *Fleet-Street Eclogues, Ballads
and Songs, The Testament of John Davidson, A Romantic*

*Farce, An Unhistorical Pastoral, Bruce: A Chronicle Play,
Scaramouch in Naxos: A Pantomime, Smith: A Tragic Farce,*
and so on. Although the title, 'Ballads and Songs' may
be unremarkable enough in the context of other late
nineteenth-century volumes of poetry, the other titles
promise the unexpected, be it the ironic combination of
the pastoral eclogue with contemporary Fleet Street, or
the archaic Testament, or the children's pantomime, or
a hybrid of tragedy and farce.

Ambivalence is often at the core of Davidson's work
as he continually adopts some traditional form and
then proceeds to dismantle and subvert all its
constituent parts. In theory he argues against any
evolutionary system in literary history:

> Because Victorian literature succeeds Georgian
> literature, ... this epoch of letters is not necessarily
> related to those as child and great-great-great-
> grandchild. I suggest that English literature is a
> forest rather than a plantation; a land of upheavals
> and disarranged strata that science can make little
> of yet, at least; and a place of meteorites of which
> the earth can tell nothing.[26]

On the contrary, we must throw off the burden of the
past: 'Literature is the greatest foe of literature. We
have jungles to cut down, gag after gag to wrench from
our mouths' before we can speak for ourselves.[27]

One of his primary objections to Victorian poetry
was its refusal to admit the world's misery, the social
and economic misery experienced by the majority.
'Poetry is not always an army on parade; sometimes it
is an army coming back from the wars, epaulettes and
pipe-clay all gone, shoeless, ragged, wounded, starved
...'[28] Playing on the Pre-Raphaelites' name for their
aesthetic revolution, Davidson called his 'Pre-
Shakespeareanism':

> All the woe of the world is to be uttered at last.

Poetry has been democratised. Nothing could prevent that. The songs are of the high-ways and the by-ways. The city slums and the deserted villages are haunted by sorrowful figures, men of power and endurance, feeding their melancholy not with heroic fable, the beauty of the moon, and the studious cloisters, but with the actual sight of the misery in which so many millions live. To this mood the vaunted sweetness and light of the ineffective apostle of culture are like a faded rose in a charnel-house, a flash of moonshine on the Dead Sea. ... It must all out. The poet is in the street, the hospital. He intends the world to know that it is out of joint. He will not let it alone. With whatever trumpet or jew's-harp he can command he will clang and buzz at its ear, disturbing its sleep, its pleasures; discoursing of darkness and of the terror that walks by night.[29]

Davidson's Utopian goal to do away with all conventional limitations, including genres — in order to describe the world in which he lived — was at odds with any form he chose. His struggle with form characterizes his work from beginning to end. If modern poetry is characterized by 'formal desperation' or 'less a style than a search for a style', as modern critics have claimed,[30] then Davidson's work is comparable to other modern writers whose break up of traditional styles and whose interest in the fragmentary have forced them to write in a new way. Davidson's search for a form adequate to his experience of the modern world began with the traditional Scottish ballad, but it also took him through the Glasgow music-halls in a poem such as 'Thirty Bob a Week'. It took him finally to his last, posthumously published volume, *Fleet Street and Other Poems*, which stands as a landmark in the breakthrough to a new kind of poetry. Here, in poems such as 'The Crystal Palace', the direction is clear: a new poetry — urban, realist, and conversational — has been achieved. The voice that finally evolves in this late poetry is an ironic one: distanced yet profoundly concerned, it watches and comments, chronicles and criticizes the contemporary world. It is, in fact, the evolved voice of his 'Random Itinerant', a figure he had invented in the early nineties, who, while residing in London, was able to weave his way around and through the metropolis, always on foot, always with adventures, observations, or fantasy discussions.[31] Davidson is known to us in the twentieth century mostly through the mythologizing of W. B. Yeats in 'The Tragic Generation' as one of the London nineties poets, or through T. S. Eliot and his admission that the clerk in Davidson's 'Thirty Bob a Week' 'haunted [him] all [his] life'.[32] Nevertheless, it may be that Davidson's Random Itinerant and his struggle with form offers a more interesting clue to Davidson's art.

NOTES

1. Fergus Ferguson, 'Biographical Sketch', in *Sermons of the Late Rev. Alexander Davidson*, Edinburgh 1893, p. xiv.
2. *The Candid Friend*, 1 June 1901, quoted in R. D. MacLeod, Introduction, *Poems and Ballaads, by John Davidson*, London 1959, p. 14.
3. A. M. Currie, 'A Biographical and Critical Study of John Davidson', unpublished thesis, B.Litt., Oxford 1953, p. 18.
4. E. Northey, 'The Poetry of John Davidson (1857–1900) in Its Social, Political and Philosophical Contexts', Ph.D. thesis, Newcastle-on-Tyne 1976, pp. 50–1.
5. Letter to A. Swinburne, 28 March 1878; printed in J. Benjamin Townsend, *John Davidson: Poet of Armageddon*, New Haven 1961, p. 48.
6. *Plays*, London 1894, p. 223.
7. In *The Pilgrimage of Strongsoul and Other Stories*, London 1896, pp. 155–212.
8. Liebich M.S., The William Andrews Clark Memorial Library, University of California, Los Angeles, p. 5.
9. Liebich, p. 4.

10. John Davidson, 'The Testament of a Juryman', *Westminster Gazette*, January 1905, p. 2; Davidson, Letter to Sir John Martin-Harvey, 30 April 1808, PUL; Townsend, p. 36; 'Mr. John Davidson', *Bookman* (London), 7 (1894), 49.

11. Edmund Gosse, *The Life of Algernon Swinburne*, New York 1917, p. 243.

12. Gosse, p. 244.

13. Townsend, p. 7.

14. In *MA*, pp. 30–41.

15. *MA*, pp. 76–156.

16. *MA*, pp. 1–29.

17. W. B. Yeats, "The Celt in London: The Rhymers' Club', *Boston Pilot*, 23 April 1892; rpt. in *Letters to the New Island*, Cambridge, Mass. 1970, p. 142.

18. Jane T. Stoddart, 'An Interview with Mr. John Davidson', *Bookman* (New York), I (February 1895), 85.

19. See letter from W. S. McCormick to Edmund Gosse, 6 December 1898, printed in part in MacLeod, pp. 34–7.

20. 'On the Downs', *Speaker*, 5 February 1898, p. 179; rpt. in *MF*, p. 248.

21. 'Court Theatre', *Times* (London), 11 January 1904, p. 11.

22. Letter, 4 January 1906, BL.

23. See Mary O'Connor, 'Did Bernard Shaw Kill John Davidson? The Tragi-Comedy of a Commissioned Play', *Shaw Review*, 21 (1978), 108–23.

24. *Fleet Street and Other Poems*, London 1909, p. [v].

25. Howard Mumford Jones, 'A Minor Prometheus', *Freeman* (New York), 25 October 1922, p. 153.

26. '*Godfrida*', *Saturday Review*, 5 November 1898, p. 609.

27. Epilogue, *MM*, p. 171.

28. 'The Criticism of Poetry', *MF*, p. 71.

29. *MF*, pp. 33–4.

30. Frank Kermode, 'The Modern', in *Modern Essays*, London 1971, p. 48; Malcolm Bradbury and James McFarlane, 'The Name and Nature of Modernism', in their *Modernism, 1890–1930*, Harmondsworth 1976, p. 29.

31. See *A Random Itinerary*, London 1894.

32. W. B. Yeats, *Autobiographies*, London 1955, pp. 315–18; T. S. Eliot, Preface, *John Davidson: A Selection of His Poems*, ed. Maurice Lindsay, London 1961, p. [xii].

CHAPTER 1

EARLY FICTION AND PLAYS

Prose Fiction

Davidson's short stories, written mostly while he was in Scotland and collected later in two volumes published in the nineties, *The Pilgrimage of Strongsoul* and *Miss Armstrong's Circumstances*, and his longer early fiction, *The North Wall* and *Perfervid*, offer a prelude to his literary career. If any collection of Davidson's works suggests a Scottish space, it is these stories. If not an actual regional writer here, Davidson is relying a good deal on Scottish places, characters, and even dialect. In 'Alison Hepburn's Exploits', the description of Edinburgh streets and parlours defines the external and internal worlds of his characters. The closed Calvinist mind is present in 'The Schoolboy's Tragedy', while the rural haunts that were precious to Davidson are present in the Ochils scenes in 'Pilgrimage of Strongsoul' and *Perfervid* and in the views of the Firth of Clyde from Gourock in *The North Wall*.

The sympathy with children discussed earlier shows up not only in 'The Schoolboy's Tragedy' but in two stories that might well be read by children: *The Pilgrimage of Strongsoul* and 'Interregnum in Fairyland'. Both combine a knowledge of the child's imagination and desire for adventure with a related blurring of the distinctions between reality and fantasy, life and literature. Pilgrim Strongsoul leaves home with *Pilgrim's Progress* tucked under his arm to journey to the Celestial City, and the story progresses through the

various delightful ironic cross-purposes that his 'real'
encounters produce. It combines all the necessary
adventures, suspense, and success that a children's story
demands with a level of ironic play for both the adult
and child reader. In 'The Interregnum in Fairyland',[1]
the young girl who is drawn into the wood to find the
fairies she has read about turns out to be the Queen of
Fairies who had been placed in hiding while an
interregnum of evil powers had usurped her authority.
The little girl, unconscious of her identity and destiny,
enjoys all the excitement of discovery and
transformation as the animals and fairies help her with
their magic to escape from and finally defeat the evil
witch and become the Queen.

The confusion of literature and life is made explicit
in Davidson's first published novel, *The North Wall*
(1885), later issued as 'The Practical Novelist' in *The
Great Men and the Practical Novelist* (1891). With some
self-conscious play with his own editors, Davidson
makes his hero into 'an unsuccessful literary man,...
who had composed dramas and philosophical romances
which no publisher, nor editor, could be got to read'.[2]
This Maxwell Lee 'refused scornfully the task of writing
"an ordinary vulgar, sentimental, and sensational story
of the kind required,"'[3] and instead took up working in
the flesh, proceeding to arrange the lives of a group of
people according to his artistic whims. This 'practical
novelist' thus explores with ironic wit the process of
writing, the relation of the artist to his characters, and
of art to life. Lee pronounces:

> Novel-writing is effete; novel-creation is about to
> begin. We shall cause a novel to take place in the
> world. We shall construct a plot; we shall select a
> hero; we shall enter into his life, and produce the
> series of events before determined on. Consider for
> a minute. We can do nothing else now. The last

development — the naturalist school, is a mere
copying, a bare photographing of life — at least
that is what it professes to be. This is not art.
There can never again be an art of novel-writing.
But there can be, there shall be, you will aid me to
begin, the art of novel-creation.[4]

Through a sleight of hand Davidson is able both to
accept the genre his audience and publishers want —
that of the comic adventure and romantic novel — and
to undermine its credibility. There is even a final
postscript (which is titled 'Prefatory') where Davidson
attacks his complacent and repressed middle-class
readers who evade life by resorting to sentimental
novels, those who are 'afraid to be alone, without
thoughts or ideas; who, whenever you have a moment of
that highest of privileges, leisure, abuse it with such a
book as this; you, whose experience is all by proxy, who
are, in fact, incapable of experience of your own: this
chapter is for you'.[5]

Unfortunately, although the idea of the novel is witty
and original, the execution is not always as inspired.
Nevertheless, Davidson's humour, especially around
certain characters, can be successful. His Mr. Alec
Dempster, 'whose voice was a reminiscence of some
mechanical sound, one couldn't exactly say which',
although a caricature, is in the best Dickensian
tradition of comic figures:

'Do you think much, Mr. Dempster'?
'Think'! exclaimed Mr. Dempster, throwing his
head back in a convolution which a burlesque actor
would have paid highly to learn the trick of.
'Yes, think', repeated Lee, with the happy,
innocent smile.
'I — I can't say I do', said Dempster, perspiring
profusely. 'I — I', he continued, making a wholly
ineffectual attempt to laugh — 'I — eh-ah —
haven't given the subject much attention. But' —

'Exactly, Mr. Dempster. I understand. I have often thought, by the way, that you unlucky fellows who inherit your money, can't enjoy it so well as we who have wrought for it'.

Now, if there was one thing Dempster objected to more than another, it was to be hurried about from subject to subject. He had just got his mind focussed to the consideration of Lee's first question, when a new distance intervened, and — he saw men as trees walking. But he must make some reply. ... [6]

Although these stories are not in themselves entirely successful, they do point to many of Davidson's traits as a writer. He is able to use the dramatist's faculty of insight and sympathy, particularly in his stories about children and those that deal with 'would-be Londoners'. He has at the centre of his artistic consciousness a sense of wit or fantasy that often is connected with a desire for subversion. On many levels, especially at the level of form, he will delight in shocking, in giving an ironic twist to whatever is expected.

Early Plays

In the most successful of his early plays, *Scaramouch in Naxos: A Pantomime*, a character steps on the stage to address the audience before the play begins:

Silenus. Gentle readers — I would fain say, hearers, but I am afraid I shall never fool it on the stage — I am very fond of Pantomimes. I don't know whether I like this one so well as I liked those which I witnessed when I was a boy. It is too pretentious, I think; too anxious to be more than a Pantomime — this play in which I am about to perform. True *Pantomime* is a good-natured nightmare. Our sense of humour is titillated and strummed, and kicked and oiled, and fustigated and stroked, and exalted and

bedevilled, and, on the whole, severely handled by
this self-same harmless incubus; and our intellects are
scoffed at. The audience, in fact, is, intellectually, a
pantaloon, on whom the Harlequin-pantomime has
no mercy. It is frivolity whipping its schoolmaster,
common-sense; the drama on its apex; art, unsexed,
and without a conscience; the reflection of the world
in a green, knotted glass. Now, I talked to the
author, and showed him that there was a certain
absence from his work of this kind of thing; but he
put his thumbs in his arm-pits, and replied with some
disdain, 'Which of the various dramatic forms of the
time may one conceive as likeliest to shoot up in the
fabulous manner of the bean-stalk, bearing on its
branches things of earth and heaven undreamt of in
philosophy? The sensational dramas? Perhaps from
them some new development of tragic art; but
Pantomime seems to be of best hope. It contains in
crude forms, humour, poetry, and romance. It is the
childhood of a new poetical comedy'. Then I saw
where he was, and said, 'God be with you', and
washed my hands of him. But I'll do my best with
my part.[7]

This combination of 'crude forms, humour, poetry,
and romance' (perhaps what George Meredith was
referring to in a letter to Davidson when he said that
he showed 'fantastical humour good in youth')[8] is
brought to bear on the story of a music-hall
entrepreneur, Scaramouch, who, motivated by
nineteenth-century commercialism, sets out to sign on
the Greek God, Bacchus, as an up-and-coming
attraction (much as the London entrepreneur, Farini,
alive to post-Darwinian interests, sent off agents around
the world to track down the the 'Missing Link'). The
humour is sustained as Scaramouch tells of his last
unsuccessful attempt when his fairy was too small for

the audience to see, and as he continues to speak in his characteristic language which is all alliteration and doubling ('Mars and martyrdom'! 'Homer and homicide', 'Oakum and orchids'). Other figures fill out the humour: a drunken Silenus or a Glaucus who wants to be immortal in order to move up in the world (so to speak). Up until now, he had only dreamed of being an earl and was ready to use his daughter for that end; now he has godhead in sight. Interwoven with this satire is an interest in the supremacy of love, as the young god forfeits his immortality to stay with his mortal lover. The real Bacchus arrives triumphantly at the end, in full pantomime glory, to set the world aright and oust the imposters. Scaramouch is banished home to England, transformed into a monkey to be exhibited from Land's End to John O' Groats. On the serious side, there is a moment of subtle irony when Ariadne is troubled and cannot remember her moment on Naxos, that is to say, her mortal love for Theseus. The play ends with a celebration of mortal love.

'Things of earth and heaven undreamt of in philosophy', says Silenus, are Davidson's matter, and yet it will be his ideas about life, indeed, his philosophical ideas, that will characterize his poems, for better or worse. In his time he was most loved for his simple lyrics celebrating nature and the countryside or for his impressionist sketches of the city, but he was really a poet of ideas. His desire to be both prophet and poet leads him eventually to his testament and tragedies, to Nietzsche and Schopenhauer, but it began with his religious upbringing and perhaps with the influence of the Spasmodic writers, as Townsend has argued.

Set beside the humorous ironies of *The North Wall* or *Scaramouch*, Davidson's *Diabolus Amans* (1885), obsessed with religious issues — whether there is a God, whether one is predestined to damnation, or whether one can be saved through love — gives us an unadulterated sense of Davidson's philosophical side. In this 'dramatic poem' Angelus (underneath, a 'Diabolus' or avowed sinner) goes on a soul-searching quest to discover whether he should continue to love an innocent, good woman. It takes us through various churchyards and the sounds of sermons, to the Alps and an encounter with a despairing double, and to a hospital in London to one who has opted for good works. The poem is really a search for God and salvation, insisting finally on a love of Nature and a belief in self. Only in this world will we find true divinity. The love interest, although a theme discussed, is not explored dramatically, and the diabolic is only alluded to, not delineated, or fleshed out, so to speak, except in a series of rejections of pastors' sermons as the main characters stand outside in the churchyards. The play ends with Donna and Angelus consumating their love by reading Virgil together, a foretaste of their many evenings of marital bliss.

Although the poem does fit into the Spasmodic tradition, there is little sense of real conflict or struggle. The characters are never rounded out, and the poetry, although rich at times, is lost in the tedium of the arguments. The drama suggested by the epigraph, 'What if the devil were a man in love', is simply never achieved. The play, *Smith: A Tragic Farce* (1888), pursues Diabolus' quest for divinity in self and love, but the sectarian controversies are left behind. Diabolus in fact splits into two figures. The dynamic Smith, a natural, common man, not of the universities, is one who has maintained the integrity of his passions, and who can love without formalities. His ideas do not stem from conformity to class dictates as do those of other characters presented in the first act. The other major figure is Hallowes, a poet who has not been able to sell his work. These two and the woman who falls in love with Smith commit suicide by the end of the play. Death is the only alternative to life in this commercial world. Hallowes sees that the drudgery of teaching, or worse, business, might pay for his physical needs, but it would destroy his creative spirit; Smith and his loved one are forbidden their love by the money and class interests of her father. These extreme grand heroic gestures, especially Smith and Magdalen's suicidal leap off the cliff at the end, in this play and elsewhere in Davidson's work, are always jarring to a twentieth-century audience, especially since he, at the same time, tries to present a realistic context — a character named 'John Smith' in a pub in the midst of Cambridge men. In these more modern moments the language of the poetry is strong and convincing: Hallowes on teaching and commerce, Smith on revolutionary action, or Hallowes on poetic ambition. A theme of language is raised as Smith cries out: 'Our language is too worn, too much abused,/ Jaded and over-spurred, wind-broken, lame, —/ The hackneyed roadster every bagman mounts'.[9] The 'Acts and Codes' of schools destroy the life in children, while the lawyers and their ilk have pigeon-hole drawers for each idea and word. With Smith, 'one must become/ Fanatic — be a wedge — a thunder-bolt,/ To smite a passage through the close-grained world'.[10]

This play, and *Scaramouch*, are perhaps Davidson's most promising dramatic productions of the 1880s. The three other plays written at that time are rather apprentice pieces even though he was to stand by them until the end. *An Unhistorical Pastoral* proves easy reading, with suitable plot and appropriate outcome, where once again young love conquers all the heavy fathers, good and bad. But the plot is too close to the many Shakespearian intrigues of lost children, disguised questers, and sudden recognition scenes. Similarly, *A Romantic Farce* is too close to its models, and our interest

wanes despite some pleasant poetic passages. Davidson
was perhaps mistaken in his evaluation of these early
plays because, although he tried to instill new ideas, he
did not sufficiently work or play with the form he had
chosen. In his ballads and later genre experiments, the
playful ironic side of his talent combined with his 'new'
ideas to create important poems.

When these early plays were collected and published
by John Lane in 1894, many critics singled out '*Bruce:
A Drama* now called more correctly "A Chronicle
Play"' for praise. William Archer, perhaps with ulterior
motives, as Townsend points out, offered it as a likely
play for the opening of a Scottish literary theatre.[11]
With Shakespeare strong in his mind, Davidson had
written a flawed but at times moving drama about the
Scottish hero and his struggle against both the English
and his own Scottish detractors. Critics today might not
hold the same opinion of the play as a whole, but it is
nevertheless marked by lyrical and dramatic moments
— Wallace's trial speech that almost mesmerizes the
English court, or, most remarkable, the view of the
Battle of Bannockburn conveyed by two observers, a
young friar and an old man. The poetry of their
descriptions communicates more of the noise and clash
of battle than any mock sword fight would have done
on centre stage:

'St. Andrew and St. George! Fight on! fight on!'
A whole year's storms let loose on one small lake
Prisoned among the mountains, rioting
Between the heathery slopes and rugged cliffs,
Dragging the water from its deepest lair,
Shaking it out like feathers on the blast;
With shock on shock of thunder; shower on shower
Of jagged and sultry lightning; banners, crests,
Of rainbows torn and streaming, tossed and flung

From panting surge to surge; where one strong
  sound,
Enduring with continuous piercing shriek
Whose pitch is ever heightened, still escapes
Wroth from the roaring war of elements;
Where mass and motion, flash and colour spin
Wrapped and confounded in their blent array:
And this all raving on a summer's morn,
With unseen larks beside the golden sun,
And merest blue above; with not a breeze
To fan the burdened rose-trees, or incense
With mimic rage the foamless rivulet,
That like a little child goes whispering
Along the woodland ways its happy thought;
Were no more wild, grotesque, fantastical,
Uncouth, unnatural — and I would think
Impossible, but for the vision here —
Than in this clamorous and unsightly war,
Where swords and lances, shields and arrows, flash,
Whistle, and clang — splintered like icicles,
Eclipsed like moons, broken like reeds, like flames —
Lewd flames that lick themselves in burning lust —
With scorpion tongues lapping the lives of men;
. . . .
Where hoofs of horses spatter brains of men,
And beat dull thunder from the shakimg sod;
Where yelling pibrochs, braying trumpets, drums,
And shouts, and shrieks, and groans, hoarse, shrill —
  a roar
That shatters hearing — echo to the sky;
Where myriad ruthless vessels, freighted full
Of proud rich blood — with images of God,
Their reasoning souls, deposed from their command —
By winds of cruel hate usurped and urged,
Are driven upon each other, split, and wrecked,
And foundered deep as hell. The air is dark
With souls. I cannot look — I cannot see.[12]

NOTES

1. In *MA*, pp. 202–48.
2. *NW*, pp. 9–10.
3. *NW*, p. 10.
4. *NW*, pp. 10–11.
5. *NW*, p. 148.
6. *NW*, pp. 28, 52–4.
7. *Plays*, Greenock 1889, pp. 131–2.
8. 21 August 1889; *The Letters of George Meredith*, ed. C.L. Hind, 3 vols., Oxford 1970, II, 977.
9. *Plays*, London 1894, p. 235.
10. *Plays* (1894), p. 230.
11. Townsend, p. 86.
12. *Plays* (1894), pp. 210–11.

CHAPTER 2

THE BALLADS

Davidson's ballads are a particularly useful illustration of his struggle with form. Having made his name with 'A Ballad of a Nun' and *Ballads and Songs*, he went on to publish *New Ballads* (1896) and *The Last Ballad and Other Poems* (1899), but he had begun his experiments with the form much earlier. (His first poem at the age of twelve was 'a sturdy ballad on the Defeat of the Moors by Ramiro, King of Spain, when under the celestial sword of St. Iago twice thirty thousand heathen fell').[1] His earliest surviving ballads are collected in his 1891 *In a Music-Hall and Other Poems* and may have been written under the influence of the Glasgow Ballad Club whose goal was 'the study of Ballads and Ballad Literature, and the production and friendly criticism of original Ballads contributed by the members, the word "ballad" being interpreted in a sense sufficiently wide to include lyrical poems'.[2] In any case, these early ballads tend toward the style of the romantic ballad, distanced in locale and time and stylized in language. They retain strong ballad measures, alliteration, internal rhyme, and a tendency to elaborate description. But they also show signs of the later more rebellious poet with a taste for ironic inversions.

Such is the case, for instance, with 'Alice' which, under the guise of an episodic ballad, parodying the 'Edward'-like unveiling of truth stanza by stanza, proceeds through stages of a strip-tease:

One from her hair the pearl-strings tore:
   She seemed as fair again;
The pearls, the only gems she wore,
   Lost all their lustre then.

A cry she cried: 'Help, help, dear love!'
   They gagged her with her lace;
Her scarf — white silk, like foaming milk —
   They bound across her face.

Pale, dumb with lust, they rent her robes;
   She thanked God for her hair.
White in the wood, unsheathed she stood,
   The only flower there.

But when she felt her nakedness,
   These wolves she clasped and clung;
Their eyes devoured her sweet distress,
   And low their laughter rung. (43–4)

The eroticism of image, metaphor, and colour scheme is embarrassingly heavy-handed, but the purpose becomes clear with the poem's unexpected shift in the seventh stanza, where the eroticism is sacrificed for open sexual awareness, self-knowledge, and union. We then see that the virgin 'whiteness' throughout the poem stood not simply in contrast to the paynims' fiery lust, but as a prelude to the 'tinted snows' as 'her shuddering body dawned' for her true love who rescues her. The shift from stylized and distanced world into a dramatic scene with certain realistic psychological overtones throws one or other world into an untenable perspective. Davidson is also caught between two worlds with his simple dialogue. Such naiveté would be appropriate if the original ballad spirit were maintained throughout the poem, but it is not. The outcries from Alice and her love — 'Help, help, dear love!' or 'Hark, Alice! Hist! I keep my tryst' — are not saved in the poem by rhythm, context, or ballad simplicity.

The romance, with its violence and passion, is one strain of the ballad that appealed to Davidson; another was the supernatural tale. In 'Thomas the Rhymer' there are two main sets of supernatural events: the marriage scene with the uninvited skeletal guests and the series of reversals in nature which Thomas reads as omens of disaster. The ballad itself seems like an excuse for these two descriptive passages; the first, with its 'odour, chill, sepulchral', 'reeking stack of bones', and 'yawning eyeless holes', is reminiscent of 'Monk' Lewis' 'Alonzo the Brave' and of Scott's 'William and Helen'. In moments of striking imagery the poem succeeds. The description of the waves evoking the expectant calm before the storm is particularly impressive — 'The sleepy waves, reluctant, poised/ Drop peacefully ashore' (37) as is that of the flood which intermingles the realms of sea and land: 'Shells gleamed by drenched flowers, tangle clung/ Like snakes about the grain' (39). Furthermore, Thomas serves as one of Davidson's first heroic outsiders. Taking his legend from Scott's *Tales of a Grandfather* or from Part II of Scott's own 'Thomas the Rhymer', Davidson sets up Thomas as the seer, poet, and madman who forecasts the woes of Scotland, against the philistine, disbelieving, and mocking Earl of March.

'The Gleeman', a third ballad of the period, also portrays a figure of the poet-outcast, but the Gleeman, although he may be other-worldly, is, like Smith or the author of the Prefatory to *A North Wall*, foremost a critic of life: 'The gleeman sang in the market-town;/ The market-folk went up and down' (44). Like Nietzsche's Zarathustra, or Davidson's later Man Forbid and the poet in the Parable to *The Testament of an Empire-Builder*, the Gleeman admonishes the market folk and is persecuted for telling the truth. The broadside ballads had developed a standard opening, with the minstrel calling attention to his song.

Davidson's Gleeman transforms a formula such as 'Come all ye and listen to my tale' into a blatant attack:

'Loose your knotted brains awhile,
    Market-people, sore bested;
Traffic palsies all your isle;
    Hear a message from the dead. (45)

The scorn Davidson felt towards the market place and the contemporary world is shown in his attack on the merchants, 'the sapless ancients', 'the dreamy girls', and the 'learned clerk with icy sneer'. The poem ends with the departure of the Gleeman and his truth, leaving only the barrenness of buying and selling lies:

He wrapped his cloak about his face,
And left the bustling market-place.
The juggler had an audience,
The mountebank drew showers of pence,
The pardoner cheapened heaven for gold:
I ween the market-folk were sold. (46)

In utter desperation the narrator breaks through the impersonal fabric of the poem and curses the market folk with their own evil.

In no way is Davidson's ballad voice the truly impersonal voice of the traditional ballad; nor is it characterized by 'singleness of intention in attempting to convey no more to the simple minded than can be taken in on one reading or hearing' that T.S. Eliot found in Rudyard Kipling.[3] Davidson's voice is personal and literary. On the other hand, the ballad provided him with a narrative structure that could contain his inspiration. It also provided traditional stories that he could invert or parody. The early work of *In a Music-Hall* hints at the kinds of reversals that Davidson would find possible within the ballad form. It also indicates his specific interests in the themes associated with that form: the tale of adventure with passionate violence, romance, and sexuality; supernaturalism; and the role of the minstrel poet as rebel and outsider.

'A Ballad in Blank Verse of the Making of a Poet', Davidson's first poem in *Ballads and Songs*, adopts the generic title 'ballad' and yet abandons all the formal criteria of the genre except the fact that it is a narrative. There are no quatrain stanzas, only verse paragraphs.

Even the title, juxtaposing as it does 'blank verse' with 'ballad', suggests some idiosyncratic genre tranformation. Davidson's reasons for calling this poem a ballad are not found in its metre and structure; they are found in certain aspects of its 'inner form',[4] its attitudes, tone, and subject matter. There is a refrain-like repetition in 'Ballad in Blank Verse' that attempts to present the poem as a tale of universal interest remote in time and place:

> For this was in the North, where Time stands still
> And Change holds holiday, where Old and New
> Welter upon the border of the world. (296)

But we have already seen how this remote place turns into a very specific description of Greenock, an industrial harbour town. In many of Davidson's ballads, even in those which retain much that is traditional, the landscape is not the 'stylized limbo'[5] of the conventional ballad, but a realistic description of a specific place.

'A Ballad in Blank Verse', Davidson's *Bildungsgedicht*, documents and thematizes the young poet's search for an appropriate subject and an appropriate audience. He moves through themes we have seen in the plays, through nature, love, and classical mythology, to prophetic seer and leader of revolutions, and finally

back to a more ninetyish position of allowing all moods
to pass through him:

No creed for me! I am a man apart:
A mouthpiece for the creeds of all the world;
A soulless life that angels may possess
Or demons haunt, wherein the foulest things
May loll at ease beside the loveliest;
A martyr for all mundane moods to tear;
The slave to every passion; and the slave
Of heat and cold, of darkness and of light;
A trembling lyre for every wind to sound. (302)

The main drama of the poem is derived from the
young poet's rejection of his father's church and
Christian values. What Davidson calls 'transvaluation'
takes place in both the form of the work and its theme,
each embodying a break with the past. His ballads do
not exude the 'regret for the past' implicit in the tone of
Thomas Hardy's ballads.[6] In fact, one might say that
Davidson chose a firmly traditional form precisely in
order to break with the tradition.

There is one other important experiment in the long
narrative poem 'A Woman and Her Son'. This poem
may be seen as a comparison piece to 'A Ballad in
Blank Verse', and in the two poems the son exorcizes
his parents. In the later poem Davidson juxtaposes the
drab monotony and squalor of a suburban street with a
death scene inside one of the houses. The passages
function not only as setting. The list of squalid details
of the sights and sounds are realistic moments in an
average suburban street. But they collide with each
other in a sequence that is not a sequence, that is
without meaningful relation. The sum total of the parts
remains the parts placed side by side. And all this at
the moment of death, as a backdrop to the rather

melodramatic search for and quarrel over meaning between a son and his dying mother. Everything comes to this crucial point: time is running out for her. The poem opens with ' "Has he come yet?" the dying women asked', and her question is repeated with increasing suspense with interspersals of the meaningless repetition of daily life outside. It is not life, but death in life:

The working-men with heavy iron tread,
The thin-shod clerks, the shopmen neat and plump
Home from the city came. On muddy beer
The melancholy mean suburban street
Grew maudlin for an hour; pianos waked
In dissonance from dreams of rusty peace,
And unpitched voices quavered tedious songs
Of sentiment infirm or nerveless mirth.

'Has he come yet?'
          'Be still or you will die!'

And when the hour of gaiety had passed,
And the poor revellers were gone to bed,
The moon among the chimneys wandering long
Escaped at last, and sadly overlooked
The waste raw land where doleful suburbs thrive.

(303)

Aside from the specific foreshadowing here of *The Waste Land*,[7] there are themes paramount in the writings of both Eliot and Davidson: the themes of urban squalor and the dissolution of meaning. Later in the poem the juxtaposition of city life outside and death inside illustrates how meaning has gone out of even the images used in the poem. At her death, the sound and events outside are listed, again juxtaposed, this time with an echo of the natural/supernatural upheavals at Duncan's murder in *Macbeth*. But here the point is that whereas life outside, the shunting of trains and the cry of the child, might have given meaning to the woman's death, they do not:

> He set his teeth, and saw his mother die.
> Outside a city-reveller's tipsy tread
> Severed the silence with a jagged rent;
> The tall lamps flickered through the sombre street,
> With yellow light hiding the stainless stars:
> In the next house a child awoke and cried;
> Far off a clank and clash of shunting trains
> Broke out and ceased, as if the fettered world
> Started and shook its irons in the night. (306)

The 'as if' remains 'as if'; the simile cannot reach a level of metaphor. Even the cries of children 'dwindled and expired'.

With hindsight and in the language of his post-1898 Materialism, Davidson spoke of his Material God and Sin and Heaven and Hell as 'the warp of myth in the loom of my poetry, giving the myth a new orientation as the weaver changes the pattern of his web'.[8] If you read the 'ballads' of the nineties as a group, you are struck by this philosophical bent — no longer the simple tales of love and adventure, or the violent or supernatural events, but rather a poet, artist, lover, nun, or workman faced with crucial moral choices. Always the hero or heroine must search out his or her destiny, his or her path toward some kind of natural divinity. 'A Ballad of Heaven', 'A Ballad of Hell', and 'A Ballad of Euthenasia' make use of our ballad expectations as well as out conventional Christian moral and mythical expectations. The traditional ballad of the lovers' suicide pact or the betrayed lover who comes back to haunt the faithless one, or the tale of the bride of death is transformed into a moral tale about the correct path toward Davidson's earthly heaven (invariably via the traditional hell). In 'A Ballad of Hell' the betrayed lover, finding herself alone in hell without her loved one, never stoops to haunting him. He is not worth haunting. Rather 'she marched across the floor of hell;/ And all the damned stood up to see'.

The devil stopped her at the brink:
　She shook him off; she cried, 'Away'!
'My dear, you have gone mad I think'.
　'I was betrayed: I will not stay'.

Across the weltering deep she ran;
　A stranger thing was never seen;
The damned stood silent to a man;
　They saw the great gulf set between.

To her it seemed a meadow fair;
　And flowers sprang up about her feet.
She entered heaven; she climbed the stair
　And knelt down at the mercy-seat.

Seraphs and saints with one great voice
　Welcomed the soul that knew not fear;
Amazed to find it could rejoice,
　Hell raised a hoarse half-human cheer. (53)

Exploiting the genre that traditionally reaches into the supernatural realm, Davidson is able to shift into the Christian mythology of heaven and hell, and thence, with broadside irony in this case, to demolish standard Christian doctrines concerning suicide, damnation, infernal punishment, and the 'great gulf set between' heaven and hell. Similarly, in 'A Ballad of Euthenasia', Davidson inverts Scott's 'William and Helen', Gottfried Bürger's 'Leonore', or the traditional 'Suffolk Miracle' in order to send his bride away from all that her present world has to offer (mere gems and princes). She accepts death as the better alternative and is rewarded with a full life of work, husband, and children.

Davidson's continual reassertion of life's common-places — love, nature, children, marriage, and, in some poems, sex — is set up in the context of an age-end world of ennui and of social injustice. All Davidson's surrogate artists (in 'A Ballad of Heaven', 'A Ballad of the Artist's Wife', 'The Ballad of a Poet Born') are driven by a desire to produce great and truthful work in a world that will not pay to keep their wives, children, or families. The sacrifices made are inevitably rewarded in the heaven of these Utopian ballads, but the hardship is of a particularly *fin-de-siècle* flavour. In 'The King's Daughter of Norway: An Age-End Ballad of Euthenasia' — the original title of 'A Ballad of Euthenasia' — the maid's distress in love is transformed into decadent ennui: '"Oh, I shall never, never wed;/ For men degenerate"'.

> The sun grows dim on heaven's brow;
>   The world's worn blood runs cold;
> Time staggers in his dotage now;
>   Nature is growing old. (83)

The preoccupation with decay and extinction in this poem, however, turns endings into new beginnings.

Death's narrow door opens into the wide space of a new life as in a Yeatsian gyre. 'A Ballad of an Artist's Wife', concerned with 'this heavy-hearted age', portrays the artist who abandons his family to live through the intense experience necessary for art, experience described in a particularly 'nineties' or decadent way.

> Passion to mould an age's art,
>   Enough to keep a century sweet,
> Was in an hour consumed; each heart
>   Lavished a life in every beat.
>
> Amazing beauty filled the looks
>   Of sleepless women; music bore
> New wonder on its wings; and books
>   Throbbed with a thought unknown before. (89)

But although Davidson's language is often that of the febrile nineties, and his tales, notably that of the Nun, would fit neatly into a list of other nineties tales of 'fallen' heroes and heroines, his ballads often overstep the bounds of decadent poetry. Davidson's art must always affirm life and its commonplaces of love and nature and self-assertion. His heroes are against the world and will survive as victor-victims in the knowledge that they have not been robbed of all. When the upstart poet sings of coy cynicism in his age-end view of the world, Davidson's older, experienced, and suffering poet rises to shame the youth, and the audience that cheered him, with his own true song of the earth. In death he is triumphant, as is the enslaved Casimir in 'The Vengeance of the Duchess'.

Davidson takes this rebellion one step further in 'A Ballad of the Exodus from Houndsditch' when it is not just an individual man-forbid (his Gleeman or poet) but rather an entire mass of people who rise up in revolution against their oppressor. The poem mixes the terms of religious and social revolution. The revolutionary pageant is on one level that of the whole of christendom, struggling under the weight of Christianity's ethos of submission, but it is also set within the realistic setting of London's working-class oppressed, suggesting, as Northey has pointed out, a more radical social change than elsewhere in Davidson's poetry.[9] Usually class or social oppression, present, for instance, in 'Thirty Bob a Week', is resolved only by the revolution of the individual; here the movement has become too large, the vision too extreme to continue, and the mass erupts in violent change.

In 'A Ballad of a Nun', Davidson's most notorious poem, this basic inversion of Christian expectations also dominates. The plot is drawn from a mediaeval miracle legend, but Davidson's reworking of the legend shocked his contemporaries. The nun in the ballad is moved by sexual desire to leave the convent in search of fulfilment, but her objective is not merely, as one critic said, to ascertain *ce que c'est un homme*.[10] Her quest is after 'knowledge', not only of man but of life, and the poem — like most of Davidson's important poems — becomes a philosophical quest. The theme of the necessary interdependence of the natural life and the religious one is reinforced by a constant interplay of imagery from the two realms. Thus 'The fittest bride of Christ' must learn to be 'sister to the mountains ... sun and moon' before she may become sister to God.

The first climax of the poem, in stanzas 22 and 23 (ll. 85–92), is both sexual and philosophical. At the moment 'she gave him all her passion's hoard', she was able to say 'this is life's great meaning'. When she returns to the convent she is greeted by the Virgin, who has taken her place as convent doorkeeper. Mary receives her, not as 'strange lady' but as 'sister, ... Sister to God'. Mary's tender actions, her kissing and blessing, and the aura about her present a vision of beauty. Although the nun had instinctively known the truth at the moment of sexual ecstacy, she is not assured of her divinity until this meeting with Mary. The Virgin blesses her, not for returning, but for leaving. Having followed her natural inclinations, she has discovered her own natural divinity. She has made the necessary submission to the physical world of which she is a part: 'She made herself one with Nature by employing her body, however blindly, for its own appointed purpose'.[11] At the second and last climax of the poem, all masks, of religious fervour, of haggard she-wolf, and finally of the Virgin, drop away and we are left in the final stanza with a renewal of the natural cycle of day and night:

'You are sister to the mountains now,
    And sister to the day and night;
Sister to God'. And on the brow
    She kissed her thrice, and left her sight.

While dreaming in her cloudy bed,
    Far in the crimson orient land,
On many a mountain's happy head
    Dawn lightly laid her rosy hand. (70)

Although Davidson's serious intentions are clear, it is not surprising that the poem was taken as self-indulgent and perhaps pornographic. Despite his denials — 'there is no indication of debauchery anywhere. ... the nun is a healthy woman'[12] — the cliché fantasy of the debauched nun negates any unqualified solemn reading of the poem. The notoriety of the poem ('No other poem appearing in the *Yellow Book* was more widely quoted than this famous ballad'[13]) was a function of the subject matter, together with the ninetyish febrile language that Davidson exploits.

In 'A Ballad of a Nun' Davidson has borrowed from the ballad its stark imagery, dramatic narrative, iambic

metre, quatrain stanza, and alternating rhyme. He also
employs an almost chiastic structure, which David
Buchan has convincingly demonstrated to be a part of
the   ballad   form.[14]   This   structure   is   repeated
throughout Davidson's ballads with variations. Here
the nun begins and ends at the convent but makes her
necessary 'fall' into the world of flesh and passionate
experience. In this peripeteia she discovers truth. In
other poems like Tannhäuser' and 'Lancelot', Davidson
begins with the 'fallen' state and proceeds through a
peripeteia of attempted reform. But the poems end
where they began, reconfirmed in their original
position. They have proved to themselves their
'appointed purpose'. Davidson's Nietzschean transvaluation is always a matter of bringing the spiritual
world into the natural, of eliminating duality. The
ballad, with its easy access to the supernatural world,
gave him the opportunity of working out this purpose.
He is always intertwining the two worlds, describing
one in terms of the other and grounding both in
physical experience.

Two interesting poems, 'The Last Ballad' and 'The
Ordeal', written during Davidson's period of crisis in
Sussex in 1897–98, show how he modulated the ballad
narrative form to deal with his own personal anguish.
At the same time he was evolving a theory of poetry
that describes the relation between art and the poet's
personal experience. In an article called 'The Art of
Poetry' (1898) he speaks of the subconscious in man
that shows itself best under the guise of dramatic form:

> Poetry is the most empirical of all the arts; in a
> sense every poet is a charlatan; he can give no
> authority except his own experience, his own
> imagination; in the last resort he can give no
> authority at all; he cannot tell: it was the Muse.
> Whether he be artificer or artist, and the true poet
> is always both, it is liberty of utterance he seeks.

Poetry is the least artificial of all the arts; it is at its best when it is most archaic. This is not a matter of obsolete words; rather it is an eschewing of libraries, a getting back to the earth divested, saving the harp and sword, of all the inventions of man's hands and mind. Thus the freest utterance is always to be found in the narrative or the drama. Subconsciousness, which the poet singing in his own character inevitably obscures — that is to say, the eternal, the voice of the species — becomes audible in personation. The Elizabethan-Jacobean age, the great period of the drama, is also the great period of poetry, when every aid to free and full utterance was employed in the disdain of art. It was in *The Spanish Tragedy* that Kyd revealed the new and excellent way of the madman. Here was liberty at last; everything could be said; and the kernel of the world appear through the rent in the heart, the crack in the mind. Hieronimo announces the woe of the awakened intelligence trembling on the verge of madness in three lines, three crude lines that are not surpassed by any piercing utterance of Hamlet, Timon, or Lear:

> This toils my body, this consumeth age,
> That only I to all men just must be,
> And neither gods nor men be just to me.

It is a cry wrung from the inmost heart. These words do not occur in the additional matter; they are Kyd's, and they are the cognisance of Elizabethan tragedy.[15]

The poet therefore begins with personal experience but he must reach a level of subconscious knowledge which is the level of the voice of the species. And the best way, the only way, to do this is through indirect expression, through drama and fiction, through perhaps the Nietzschean dramatic mask.

'The Last Ballad' and 'The Ordeal' illustrate two different solutions to the search for an appropriate form and dramatic voice. 'The Ordeal' is a mediaeval dramatic tale told in blank verse. Hilary accuses his wife of adultery and brings her before the king and the law. Both Bertha and Godfrey plead their innocence and also agree to trials by ordeal, but they both die in the test. Godfrey's failure and death in the joust, like Bertha's death on the ploughshares, is a sign not of adultery but rather of the impossibility of miracles — that is, that there is no law superior to natural law. Godfrey's quest for the Phoenix ends in death, but the related imagery surrounding Bertha's death — the fire and ashes, and the story born on the wind to mariners afar — suggests that this spiritual quest has been transferred to Bertha's love. Again, although thwarting our expectations, Davidson goes beyond a simple moral of true love triumphing or God rewarding the just. On the level of the plot, evil is the victor: 'harlots and the prodigals / Jested and danced about the blazing corpse.' But on another level the story of Bertha and Godfrey will be told. At the end of the poem the imagery achieves the quality and power of a fine ballad:

And, fresh with scent of meadow-hay new-reaped,
The land-breeze bore to many a mariner,
Outward or homeward bound, the sweetest news,
Across the sounding threshold of the sea. (324)

The poem speaks of a natural world and opposes this to institutional laws, whether man-made or ordained by God. The theme is developed in the references to language: to silence; to lies; to legal pleading and sentencing; to the voice of God or the harsh, devilish voice of Hilary; to tales, romances, and news. There is a scale of value which situates the sentence of the law and the voice of God and the devil together with the rabble's cries for blood on one side; and, on the other, the tale and the romance with the sound of larks and blackbirds, and 'the sweetest news,/ Across the sounding threshold of the sea'. The two kinds of language ironically counterpoint each other, as Hilary scornfully attacks Bertha's passionate account of her love as 'a perfect tale/ A plot nicely prepared' or 'a magpie tale', and, with equal scorn, Godfrey's account of his quest for the Phoenix as a 'romance'. All language which reflects the law turns out to be a set of lies. God's voice is 'tigrish clamour' and leads ultimately to the gnashing and roaring of the harlots, prodigals, ballad-mongers, and market-haunters. Although Bertha's and Godfrey's true, passionate monologues are accused of being lies, artificial, fabricated tales and romances, it is these that persist beyond the voice of law and even Bertha's failure. Her 'fairy-tale', with its happy ending, told to her children, is in part redeemed; she lives on, and her passion and truth live on in the news carried across the sea — in other words, in the ballad tale which has just been told.

'The Last Ballad' finds its dramatic voice, its 'personation', in the figure of Lancelot. The conflict between the traditional ballad framework and the need to express a personal 'cry wrung from the inmost heart' is apparent in the pressure of syntax on the verse line, metre, and quatrain, and in the invasion of realistic description. Davidson's concerns in this poem, written in September and October 1898, lead him far from the popular ballad form with its impersonal narrator, its stark outline of action, and even from the strong elemental passions evoked in his earlier ballads. Here Davidson dwells on Lancelot's complex emotional state and metaphysical dilemma.

The narrative structure of the poem, like that of 'A

Ballad of a Nun' and 'The Ballad of Tannhäuser', is
cyclical, and stems from a logic inherent in Davidson's
vision of the experience rather than from any
chronological sequence in Malory's story.[16] For
instance, within the dramatic context of Lancelot's
struggle, the retelling of his meeting with Elaine
coincides with a psychological need to expurgate the
guilt from his mind. The poem opens with Lancelot's
fulfilling his role as Arthur's champion, but secretly
inspired by his love for Guinevere. The successful
interaction between his work and his love is rendered in
the beautiful meshing of images from the field of battle
to the field of love. The sheaves of spray in the tempest
waters elicit visions of the loosened tresses of her hair,
and the pungent odours of the battlefield are refined by
her violet breath:

> In passages of gulfs and sounds,
>   When wild winds dug the sailor's grave,
> When clouds and billows merged their bounds,
>   And the keel climbed the slippery wave,
>
> A sweet sigh laced the tempest; nay,
>   Low at his ear he heard her speak;
> Among the hurtling sheaves of spray
>   Her loosened tresses swept his cheek.
>
> And in the revelry of death,
>   If human greed of slaughter cast
> Remorse aside, a violet breath,
>   The incense of her being passed
>
> Across his soul, and deeply swayed
>   The fount of pity; o'er the strife
> He curbed the lightning of his blade,
>   And gave the foe his forfeit life. (136)

However, the opening stanza had already hinted at
Lancelot's uneasy state. The images of banishment and

sterility place him beyond the pale:

> By coasts where scalding deserts reek,
>> The apanages of despair;
> In outland wilds, by firth and creek,
>> O'er icy bournes of silver air. (135)

An attempt to see Guinevere is stopped by the sight of the 'sky that canopied, the tide that girdled' her, images which confine her and define her world — to the exclusion of Lancelot. His mistaken disgust at his 'noxious lust' produces Iago-like images of the slaughter of flesh — on the battlefield, in the market-place, at the table, and in bed — climaxing in a total rejection of the senses and of sense. His Savage Man's life in the forest introduces him to the worlds of isolation, evil, madness, and despair. Lancelot's journey to the underworld and his confrontation with death culminate in the evocative 'world-old sound/ Of inarticulate despair'. The following stanza returns to a ballad tone, succinct and understated:

> Sir Lancelot, beloved of men!
>> The ancient earth gat hold of him;
> A year was blotted from his ken
>> In the enchanted forest dim. (138)

And here, structurally, the poem moves into a new ballad. The season changes and with it the place and mood of the poem. Scene-setting in the traditional ballad is usually a matter of a few lines, as in 'Bonny Barbara Allan' ('It was in and about the Martinmus time,/ When the green leaves were afalling'),[17] or more, but the pattern is identical: the season or month is specified and illustrated by details from Nature's aspect. In 'The Last Ballad' the specific time is Easter, and the phrases which follow fill out the setting with naturalistic details. However, the specific description which usually simply reinforces the general aspect of summer here becomes complicated realistic representation.

At Easter when the thorn beset
    The bronzing wood with silver sprays,
And hyacinth and violet
    Empurpled all the russet ways;

When buttercup and daffodil
    A stainless treasure-trove unrolled,
And cowslips had begun to fill
    Their chalices with sweeter gold,

He heard a sound of summer rush
    By swarthy grove and kindled lawn;
He heard, he sighed to hear the thrush
    Singing alone before the dawn. (138)

Davidson borrowed this passage from his prose essay
'Chanctonbury Ring', a travel sketch of a real place in
Sussex.[18] His images are too intricate to be contained
in a single verse line, and the effect is of the eye
scanning a real landscape. It becomes clear as Lancelot
moves out of the wood and up the hill that the scene-
setting is intricately linked with his state of mind. The
scenery of the Sussex Downs, used here and elsewhere
in Davidson's work, has acquired symbolic value.

Just as the ballad imagery gives way under the
poem's emotional weight, the ballad verse line is broken
in moments of intense psychological drama. In stanza
49 the first line carries over from stanza 48 to complete
the vision of the advancing Galahad:

            on the burnished road
The milkwhite steed, the dazzling mail

Advanced and flamed against the wind;
    And Lancelot, his body rent
With the fierce trial of his mind
    To know, reeled down the steep descent. (139)

All the ballad rules of metre and line phrase are
abandoned in order to accommodate the physical and

mental anguish of Lancelot. The line breaks reinforce the reader's sense of Lancelot's agony ('rent') and struggle ('mind/ To know'). He strains to know not merely who advances, but to understand the meaning, to know finally the self and the universe. The climax at this point cannot be contained in the ballad stanza:

Sir Lancelot a moment hung
  In doubt, then knelt and made an end
    Of all his madness, tensely strung

In one last effort to be free
    Of evil things that wait for men
In secret, strangle memory,
    And shut the soul up in their den. (140)

The efforts and struggles of the poem up until now culminate in this Promethean effort to throw off the 'evil things that wait for men/ In secret, strangle memory.' And again the line-breaks convey Lancelot's struggle.

Galahad is able to free Lancelot from his guilt-locked memory and offer him the long-needed human contact: he 'clothed his heart in human garniture once more.' However, Galahad's vision of the Holy Grail will not suffice. Described in ethereal terms, with images of sound rather than touch, it offers a spirituality that Lancelot will reject. This last conversion in the poem — from the vision of the Holy Grail back to his own vision of Guinevere — we sense as right and inevitable. Since the vision of the Queen returns to him in spite of his resolve and his former anguish, it cannot be denied. Lancelot returns to his life of action, again reinforced by his personal vision. The poem returns to its beginning, but without the anxiety and severity which inspired the opening stanza.

In a short announcement drawn up for John Lane to precede the publication of *The Last Ballad and Other*

Poems, Davidson wrote, 'The meaning of the ballad ['The Last Ballad']... is simply that there are those who follow the Holy Grail and those who do not, those who can and those who cannot; and Mr. Davidson thinks that is the last word on the matter the poet is entitled to speak, leaving the criticism of conduct to others'.[19] 'The Last Ballad', like 'A Ballad of a Nun', 'A Ballad of Tannhäuser', and 'The Ordeal', has shifted its quest from the spiritual realm to the natural world. 'God', the Phoenix, or the Holy Grail must be found in the love of a man and a woman. Lancelot's abandonment of the Holy Grail and Godfrey's loss of the Phoenix leave us not with a pessimistic capitulation, but with a faith in the physical world which will eventually lead to a more vigorous affirmation in Davidson's later Materialism.

With 'The Last Ballad' Davidson has reached the limits of the ballad form. The poem gains strength from the personal anguish and the metaphysical and moral dilemmas that Davidson needed to write about at this time. The conflict between these and the impersonal narrative of the ballad adds to its vitality. The poem abandons any attempt to portray a dramatic struggle between two characters, and transfers the conflict to the warring factions in Lancelot's mind. The other characters in the poem, whether they appear (Galahad) or not (Guinevere, Elaine, and Arthur), function entirely within the hero's mind. The dialogue is thus transformed into soliloquy or emotional outburst. The deviations from the ballad, enforcing as they do the psychological state of Lancelot, make this one of Davidson's finest poems. It is the very moment where the ballad form fails Davidson that it provides the best vehicle for expression.

At the same time, the deviations also indicate that Davidson is searching for a different kind of form. The run-on lines, run-on stanzas, and caesuras all point to the need for something other than the ballad quatrain, verse line, and rhyme. The success of 'The Ordeal' suggests that the blank verse paragraph is a more suitable medium for Davidson's 'personation' and 'cry... from the inmost heart'. Although the ballad had provided Davidson with a form of control and a process of transforming both convictions and personal experience into legend, it would rarely contain the 'high' matters of his thought and experience. Only blank verse, in drama or monologue, would now suffice.

There is one last anomaly that needs mention. Davidson returned to the ballad once more in the last decade of his life and succeeded, as other critics have noted, to create technically one of his best ballads. In 'A Runnable Stag', first published as 'A Ballad of a Runnable Stag', the themes have not changed. Davidson is still dealing with the oppressed victim who must, through his own assertion, and acceptance of death, rise to the status of victor. But in this case Davidson has controlled his allegory and exploited the rhythm to carry the drama of the poem from beginning to end:

When the pods went pop on the broom, green broom,
  And apples began to be golden-skinned,
We harboured a stag in the Priory coomb,
  And we feathered his trail up-wind, up-wind,
  We feathered his trail up-wind —
    A stag of warrant, a stag, a stag,
    A runnable stag, a kingly crop,
    Brow, bay and tray and three on top,
    A stag, a runnable stag.

. . . .

When he turned at bay in the leafy gloom,
  In the emerald gloom where the brook ran deep,
He heard in the distance the rollers boom,

And he saw in a vision of peaceful sleep,
In a wonderful vision of sleep,
    A stag of warrant, a stag, a stag,
    A runnable stag in a jewelled bed,
    Under the sheltering ocean dead,
    A stag, a runnable stag.

So a fateful hope lit up his eye,
    And he opened his nostrils wide again,
And he tossed his branching antlers high
    As he headed the hunt down the Charlock glen,
    As he raced down the echoing glen
        For five miles more, the stag, the stag,
        For twenty miles, and five and five,
        Not to be caught now, dead or alive,
        The stag, the runnable stag. (159–61)

NOTES

1. 'Mr. John Davidson', *Bookman* (London), 7 (1894), 48.
2. Henry Johnston, Memoir, in *Ballads and Other Poems*, by William Freeland, Glasgow 1904, p. xxii.
3. T. S. Eliot, 'Rudyard Kipling', *A Choice of Kipling's Verse*, London 1941, p. 10.
4. René Wellek and Austin Warren, *Theory of Literature*, 3rd ed., New York 1956, p. 231.
5. David Buchan, *The Ballad and the Folk*, London 1972, p. 76.
6. See Thom Gunn, 'Hardy and the Ballads', *Agenda*, 10 (1972), 33.
7. Pointed out by J. A. V. Chapple, *Documentary and Imaginative Literature, 1880–1920*, London 1970, p. 118.
8. *Theatrocrat*, pp. 32–3.
9. Northey, p. 125 ff.
10. Arthur Quiller-Couch, *Adventures in Criticism*, Cambridge 1924, p. 176.
11. Letter to William Archer, 26 October 1894, BL; quoted in Townsend, p. 500.
12. Letter from Davidson to Grant Richards, 29 November 1894, PUL; quoted in *Poems*, p. 485.
13. Katherin Lyon Mix, *A Study in Yellow: The 'Yellow Book' and Its Contributors*, Lawrence, Kansas 1950, p. 116.
14. Buchan, p. 100.

15. 'The Art of Poetry', *MF*, pp. 127–8.
16. The 'facts' in Davidson's poems are taken from the *Morte d'Arthur*, Books XI–XIII, ch. x.
17. *English and Scottish Popular Ballads*, ed. Francis James Child, 5 vols., New York 1965, II, 276.
18. 'Chanctonbury Ring', *Speaker* (Supp), 30 April 1898, pp. 553–4.
19. MS enclosed in a letter to John Lane, 5 January 1899, Sir Allen Lane Collection.

CHAPTER 3

THE MUSIC-HALL POEMS

In 1892, when W. B. Yeats gave an account of the contemporary literary scene in London, he chose to illustrate his point with two new volumes of poetry, one by Arthur Symons, the other by Davidson. *In a Music-Hall and Other Poems* was an example, said Yeats, of the new wave of writers who searched 'for new subject matter, new emotions'.[1] Other critics would describe Davidson as a forerunner in a renaissance in poetry which 'scouted the obviously beautiful, the palpably romantic, and dealt instead with the actual circumstances of the poets' lives .... Now artists, instead of gazing into the past, looked with wondering and enraptured eyes on things actually around them, and accordingly, handled themes which had long been thought artistically useless'.[2] Yeats argued that the search for new subject matter was a reaction to the 'search for new forms merely, which distinguished the generation now going out'.[3] In Davidson's case the music-hall poems were not only a venture into new subject matter but a significant experiment with a new form, the popular working-class genre of the music-hall song. This version of the dramatic monologue, a descendant of the broadside ballad, presents a character who introduces his life and situation through song, often humorous, sometimes sentimental. Davidson was able to exploit the dramatic possibilities of character and the speaking voice, integrating language and situation to create one of his best poems, 'Thirty Bob a Week'. Just as the ballad had allowed Davidson to use its supernatural themes, so the music-hall song opened up the world of the city and the contemporary scene. Whereas Lancelot and Thomas Rhymer offered Davidson personations for the ballads, music-hall singers and clerks fill his music-hall poems with convenient contemporary masks.

His earliest monologues relied on Browning's psychological insights and use of irony. 'The Rev. E. Kirk, B.D.' is a minor and cruder version of 'My Last Duchess'. The country parson guides his guest through the manse, dropping the names of his powerful friends, pointing out his worldly possessions, mentioning by the way how much money he makes in a year. All the while he is unaware of his culpable complacency. Davidson gives him religious metaphors to describe his secular wealth, thus emphasizing his spiritual poverty. The pastor calls his manse a 'rambling Tower of Babel ... with every fruit in the gable' (29). His 'solid steeple' is included with his 'other earthly prizes' and is ironically set '*between* me and the sky' (emphasis added). There is a moment when the parson seems about to turn to some consideration of his parishioners: 'The sheep are few', he says, 'somehow to God I'll answer how I fed mine ...' but breaks off here with an ellipsis. He then returns to his real concerns, and the stanza concludes: 'And there's my gallant salmon-rod, and there my famous red-line'. A man who sees all things as 'no deadly matter' is appropriately presented in tripping rhythms and simple rhymes. The poem progresses from the sparse and officious title, perhaps his calling card, to an intimate summary of his attributes: 'one ... on the sunny side of thirty and an athlete'. The entire poem has been a mercenary advertisement for his body and property.

'Ayrshire Jock', a monologue of the same period, is also a poem in which the speaker presents himself to his auditor, giving a description and assessment of his character and profession. However, the complexity here stems from a basic insecurity felt by the character about his own identity. Where the Rev. Kirk was oblivious to the implications of his position, Ayrshire Jock's awareness is evident in his own stumblings and contrarieties as he reviews his life, his former ambitions, his compromises, and his present penurious and slightly intoxicated state. The poem ironically begins with the assurance of a legal document: 'I John Auld, in my garret here,/ In Sauchiehall Street, Glasgow, write ...' (11). The assurance is soon deflated as John Auld's struggle is dramatically unveiled. The insistence of the legal form turns out to be only a prop. John Auld not only happens to be writing at this moment, he also writes for a living; and the poem will be about the difficulties, the impossible position, of a Glaswegian poet. How does this Scottish poet, 'like many another lad from Ayr', survive in the city, forced into writing books for money? Born into the Burnsian tradition, to a decaying dialect, to illusions of grandeur, he nevertheless has to face the realities of urban experience. He does not write but is destined to 'scribble' with diluted ink and a splay-footed pen by meagre light and minimum heat. It is significant that the poem comes alive at moments which are closest to the experience of the Glaswegian poet behind Ayrshire Jock. Davidson, like Auld, chose to write within the English tradition:

> I rhymed in English, catching tones
> From Shelley and his great successors;
>   Then in reply to written groans,
> There came kind letters from professors. (13)

Davidson's experience with John Nicol, Swinburne, and Meredith gives strength to the ironic tone of these lines, to the cold anger of the failed artist's wit. But the economic reality remains dominant. He has made his minimum income but will never be a critical success. Enticing memories of childhood and lost chances are now mere ghosts in a Mariana world where life is only present through its absence:

Ghosts lurk about the glimmering room,
    And scarce-heard whispers hoarsely fall:
I fear no more the rustling gloom,
    Nor shadows moving on the wall;
    For I have met at church and stall,
In streets and road, in graveyards dreary,
    The quick and dead, and know them all:
Nor sight nor sound can make me eerie.
. . . .
I'll draw the blind and shut — alas!
    No shutters here! ... My waning sight
Sees through the naked windows pass
    A vision. Far within the night
    A rough-cast cottage, creamy white,
With drooping eaves that need no gutters,
    Flashes its bronze thatch in the light,
And flaps its old-style, sea-green shutters.

There I was born. ... I'll turn my back. ... (12)

The memories are punctuated with Jock's satisfied salutes to his Scottish whisky. These salutations attempt to obliterate the humiliation, the disillusionment, and the ideals of his past, but the battle continues. The ghost of his past surfaces again in the last stanza and is, in turn, silenced with 'one more glass of whisky toddy'.

'In a Music-Hall' is made up of a prologue and epilogue and six dramatic monologues of music-hall artistes. The poem begins with another Glaswegian poet, this time in ''Eighty-four'. Working as a junior clerk, he abandoned his literary endeavours and

I did as my desk-fellows did;
With a pipe and a tankard of beer,

> In a music-hall, rancid and hot,
> I lost my soul night after night. (22)

This poet-clerk persona introduces the six music-hall artistes, three men and three women, without any flourish and yet with some sense of a stage presentation, imitating, as it were, the music-hall context itself:

> Some 'artists' I met at the bar,
> And others elsewhere; and, behold,
> Here are the six I knew well. (22)

The poet as music-hall 'chairman' or master of ceremonies invites us to listen to these dramatic monologues as if they were 'five-minute turns' on the stage. The poem's structure is based on the successive acts of self-presentation or revelation of these characters. All are concerned with the music hall as a moulding force in their lives, and some have conformed better than others. Some re-enact the struggle with this environment in the monologue. Others have conformed only too well, and the language, metre, verse line, and diction, as well as the content of the monologues manifest the harmony felt with the music-hall audience. Like Joyce's Dubliners, they are all in their own way paralyzed.

Those artists who have substituted a public for a personal self are given monologues that are most like music-hall turns. Tom Jenks and Julian Aragon might well be speaking from the stage. Tom Jenks comes on in full force with jogging anapaests, announcing himself entirely in terms of appearances:

> A fur-collared coat and a stick and a ring,
>   And a chimney-pot hat to the side — that's me!
> I'm a music-hall singer that never could sing;
>   I'm a sort of a fellow like that, do you see? (23)

Being a 'music-hall singer that never could sing', he has

developed the art of gesture and surface:

> So I practised my entrance — a kind of half-moon,
>   With a flourishing stride and a bow to a T,
> And the bark and the yelp at the end of the tune,
>   The principal things in my biz., do you see? (24)

The bark and the yelp dramatically account for most of the doggerel, the fumbling with the anapaests, and the grammatical confusion in his monologue. What we have is not so much the vitality of an individual personality as the strength of sheer exhibitionism. Linguistic idiosyncrasies which might have conveyed the kind of depth of character of the Thirty-Bob-a-Week clerk here only underline the 'singer without a voice'. Davidson's ironic manipulation of the language prevents us from moving behind the words to any sense of real character. 'The sort of the kind of a pluck that's mine' is the very ingredient which both condemns and enlivens this world of the music hall.

Davidson's use of illustrative failure is equally daring in 'Julian Aragon', which begins with 'Ha, ha, ha! ho, ho, ho! hee, hee, hique!/ I'm the famous Californian Comique!' He offers a different, but equal form of wish-fulfilment, boasting at the end about his easy money and women. He has more finesse and 'artistry' than Jenks, and although he insists, 'My gestures, not my words, say what I mean', his song too conveys meaning. Both the muscular contortions and smooth movement of his stage performances are conveyed in the syntax, rhythm, and words of the lines:

> I twist, contort, distort, and rage and rustle;
> I constrain my every limb and every muscle.
>   I'm limber, I'm Antaean,
>   I chant the devil's paean,
> I fill the stage with rich infernal bustle. (27)

By contrast, Mary-Jane MacPherson — a respectable governess who turned music-hall singer under financial pressures — does not have a public voice. She speaks more privately, perhaps to herself, through a series of doubts, reminiscences, and rhetorical preaching. Her manifesto, in fact, delights, as Davidson's ballads do, in the startling inversion of Christian doctrine, but character and philosophy are detached from one another here, primarily because Davidson does not establish a distinctive language for Mary-Jane in the first stanzas, a language that would carry us through *her* philosophical expositions.

Lily Dale has not been soured by the music hall as has Mary-Jane. Nor is she in absolute harmony with it as are Aragon and Jenks. One of the most effective in the sequence, Lily Dale's monologue is felt as a private conversation containing elements of a public performance as well. She is first presented in the third person ('She's thirty, this feminine cove'), and there is a great deal of masculine bravado as she 'guys' her men as if on stage. But she engages her individual auditor (presumably, the poet, and one wonders if he met her at the bar 'or elsewhere'), and wins him with her frankness and *joie de vivre*. He is there to be seduced, and she addresses him directly as a man:

> I can't sing a bit, I can't shout;
>> But I go through my songs with a birr;
> And I always contrive to bring out
>> The meaning that tickles you, sir. (24)

Her professional and personal characters both become evident in her action. As she brags and chaffs in her colloquial language, she comes alive just as the Thirty-Bob-a-Week clerk will with his idiomatic speech. There is a real interaction between speaker and auditor, between female and male: 'But I'm plump, and my legs — do you doubt me?' seems an invitation to look and almost to touch. The last stanza brings the dramatic immediacy of character and profession to a clever conclusion. Her confidence in her profession and life begins to disintegrate as she contemplates alternatives. Without breaking down, she reveals her vulnerability and in the same breath shows how she saves herself. And all the while the man listening is very much involved and implicated:

> But sometimes wild eyes will grow tame,
>> And a voice have a tone — ah, you men! —
> And a beard please me — oh, there's my name!
>> Well? I take a week's holiday then. (25)

The monologue is interrupted, appropriately, by the call-boy. 'Oh, there's my name' is part of the dramatic situation, but it also refers symbolically to the question of her 'good name' implied in the adjacent stanza, and to the profession of public performer which she has chosen.

Stanley Trafford, the failed idealist poet turned pragmatic 'Sentimental Star', introduces himself in the third person, a variation on the 'Lily Dale' opening. Constantly seeing himself through the eyes of some audience, he begins:

> This of me it may well be said —
>> Of a host as well as me:
> 'He held himself as great; he made
>> His genius his own protégé'. (25)

Paralleling Lily Dale's monologue, Trafford's leads to a moment of truth, penetrating the façade of his public life to personal anguish. But it is only for a moment. Since the show must go on, the performer regains his public self. He returns with bravado to the carefree, tinsel-clad oblivion of his music-hall life:

> And then, oh, then! Houp-la! Just so!
>> Selene, Lily, Mary-Jane?

C

With which, I wonder, shall I go
    And drown it all in bad champagne? (26)

Although 'Selene Eden' does not speak with the
colloquial realism of the others, she, the seductive
dancer, is not presented, as she might have been in a
poem by Arthur Symons, as a temptress behind a veil.
She describes her dance, imitating its mystery and
seductiveness, but she also reveals her conscious aim to
manipulate the audience. Any idea of Selene's
'chastity', innocence, or naïveté is dispelled when we
hear how she consciously leads her audience on, for she
is mistress of what Symons calls 'the science of
concupiscence'. It is a song of jewels and veils, but it is
always conscious of the lustful crowd:

But now I fill the widest stage
    Alone, unveiled, without a song;
And still with mystery I engage
    The aching senses of the throng.

. . . .

I glide, I trip, I run, I spin,
    Lapped in the lime-light's aureole.
Hushed are the voices, hushed the din,
    I see men's eyes like glowing coal. (26)

Although Davidson's poems were said to usher in the
new movement of the nineties, they have a rawness that
is rarely associated with the art of that period. Yeats
was the first to comment on the realism of 'In a Music-
Hall': 'The din and glitter one feels were far too near
the writer. He has not been able to cast them back in
imaginative dimness and distances'.[4] What must have
been striking to most readers of the time was the
language as much as the context. The poem is set in
the prosaic world of 'biz.', 'clockwork', 'drapers',
'managers', 'lime-juice cordial', and 'twenty-guineas
every week'. The imaginative dimness that Yeats called

for has purposely been eschewed for the immediacy of the accidents of life. In 'the haunting and wonderful Selene Eden', as Yeats referred to the poem, Davidson is most like Symons. But even this monologue is inspired by an atmosphere different from the London West End music halls. The point of view in the whole poem, as well as 'Selene Eden', is not the single viewer's (the enthralled voyeur's in his box). It shifts from that of serio-comique to dancer, from lion-comique to sentimental star, from male to female, from singer to audience. The dramatic monologue, as a form, allows Davidson to pick up the spoken accents of the various characters who make up the music hall: the guying of the men by Lily Dale, the clichés and meaningless phrases of Tom Jenks, and the brash manipulative casuistry of Julian Aragon.

Davidson himself had worked as a clerk in Glasgow in 1884, and at the same time was writing and trying to publish his works. Although 'In a Music-Hall' may not be aesthetically as rewarding as it might, it is an experiment in form that sent Davidson on to better work. The 'poet' of the prologue complains of the mindless work from ten to six and the lethargy of his evenings, when all ambition and literary interests have disappeared. The passivity is mirrored in the lack of polish in this part of the poem. There is no rhyme and a seemingly arbitrary shift in stanza forms. In the Epilogue the resolutions are presented in a complicated combination of terza rima, couplet, and chiastic sestet. The transition comes when the 'poet' says, 'It is better to lose one's soul, than never to stake it at all'. He then presents as the one achievement of this period his acquaintance with some artistes. By the end he is able to say, 'When I had sung them out/ I recovered my soul that was lost'. The allusion to the parable of the Good Samaritan in the epigraph of the poem, 'Who is thy neighbour?', does not refer so much to ethics as to poetics. The parable argues against isolationist ethics and, for the artist, this principle could be translated into the need for action. The contemplative world of reading novels, poems and plays is abandoned in favour of a voyage into a world of experience. Through sympathetic imagination Davidson moves out into the world of the artistes, returning with a new sense of himself.

The peculiar syntax of 'When I had sung them out' points to the complicated solution to Davidson's artistic problems at this time. The poet and the artistes are brought together in a unique formal structure. Although the main body of the poem is clearly a sequence of six dramatic monologues, the poem as a whole presents other generic features. The artistes' monologues are framed by the Prologue and Epilogue of our 'poet', who is recounting his personal experience of the music hall. The poem begins as narrative with 'In Glasgow, in 'Eighty-four', but the tale becomes drama as the six artistes re-enact the encounters that constitute the poet's experience. The poet and his tale fade as, one by one, the other individuals take the stage. These characters are not a community. There is no conscious interaction between them, and isolation itself becomes a theme of the poem as a whole. The interaction that does exist is on the level of theme, image, and language structure as some artistes trace their fall from the idealism of their youth to the inevitable pragmatism of the commercial music hall, or as oppositions are set up in the monologues between individual and society, public and private selves, heaven and hell, business and song. They are all products of their roles in the music hall.

The poet's voice in the Epilogue redirects the reader to this unity within the poem as a whole, especially as he too is concerned with the 'loss of my soul', with idealism, and with dreams. The six monologues, seen as a unit and through the perspective of this poet, invite us to discern the pattern found in life in the music hall. Random notes on random characters from that life become a revealing experience for the poet. His moving from an introspective world of novels, poems, and plays out into the seemingly selfless world of the music hall has resulted in creation. His sympathetic voyage outwards produced the monologues of his poem. Issues such as commercialism, salvation, hell or heaven on earth now become part of a greater pattern. The artistes' monologues are multiple voices expressing variations on the main theme.

Although Davidson never again turned to the music hall for the setting or content of his poems, its influence is still evident in some poems of the nineties. Shortly before 'Thirty Bob a Week' appeared, Davidson published two poems under the general title, 'To the Street Piano'. Both poems are written to the tune of popular airs: 'Ta-ra-ra-boom-de-ay' and 'After the Ball'. Aware of the sentimental tendencies of music-hall songs, he turns these romantic tunes into realist statements. The first transforms the flirtatious young girl of the famous music-hall song into a mother of three and wife of a drunkard. The second turns musings about heartache after a ball into materialist speculations about total extinction after the end of the world. 'After the Ball' might have succeeded strictly as a parody of a music-hall song, but the burden of its pessimistic philosophy is too weighty for this particular music-hall tune. These two poems are of interest primarily as five-finger exercises in the genre and as illustrations of Davidson's tendency to transform radically whatever genre he employs.

The transition from music-hall sentiment to philosophy is eminently successful, however, in 'Thirty Bob a Week'. The speaker of this monologue can say of his 'missis':

... you never hear her do a growl or whine,
　　For she's made of flint and roses, very odd;
And I've got to cut my meaning rather fine,
　　Or I'd blubber, for I'm made of greens and sod.

(63)

But he can also end up talking of evolution and the
origins of life. The continuity is assured by the
distinctive voice of the speaker, whose tone is consistent
and therefore convincing. Lines such as 'So p'r'aps we
are in Hell for all that I can tell,/ And lost and damn'd
and served up hot to God' keep metaphysics well
within the realm of the Cockney clerk's world.

The clerk introduces himself as Costermonger Joe
might have done — comically, self-deprecatingly, and
taking a bow:

I couldn't touch a stop and turn a screw,
　　And set the blooming world a-work for me,
Like such as cut their teeth — I hope, like you —
　　On the handle of a skeleton gold key;
I cut mine on a leek, which I eat it every week:
　　I'm a clerk at thirty bob as you can see. (63)

The last line gives his 'title', but the first five have
already identified his class, character, and state of
mind, and they have done so through distinctive
speech. Cliché, rhythm, and luxuriant idiomatic
expression begin to convey the passion that will grow
into anger and subside into philosophical
understanding. The influence of the music-hall genre is
evident in the realistic details, the Cockney idiom, the
ironic inversions, and the immediate and intimate
rapport with the audience. Davidson recognizes the
power of this music-hall model and uses its humour, its
language, its realism, and its typical persona as a
springboard for his own insight into the world of this
clerk.

It is dramatically appropriate that the clerk should turn to the popular forms of expression available to his own class, for his aim is to make us understand his plight. He describes himself in contrast to his auditor, Mr. Silver-tongue, whose ease of circumstance, culture, and well-established place in society are alien to the clerk, but may be supposed to be familiar to or shared by his audience (the readers of the *Yellow Book*).[5] The use of this comparison as a means of self-definition is appropriate enough since the newly-emerging lower middle class came closest to defining itself through its aspirations towards middle-class culture and respectability. Unlike the clerk, Mr. Silver-tongue has the leisure time and money to pursue the arts ('to touch a stop and turn a screw'). 'Thirty Bob a Week' is about the clerk's struggle to formulate his own experience in his state of semi-literacy. It is about the literary and philosophical aspirations of a clerk.

The poem is dramatic in the interaction between the clerk and Mr. Silver-tongue and also in the clerk's struggle to find the right expression, to formulate and convey his personal philosophy. The poem is about the 'rummiest start' of thirty bob a week (considered a very low salary at the turn of the century for a clerk with a family).[6] The clerk succeeds in conveying the dullness, the monotony, and the depersonalization felt in his world of turn-of-the-century London, on its underground, and in its suburbs. From the title on, we are in a world of wages, rooms to let, strikes and lotteries, leeks and greens and sod. The poem keeps returning to the question of money, while the animal and food imagery conveys the sense of reduction that the clerk is feeling:

> For like a mole I journey in the dark,
>   A-travelling along the underground
> From my Pillar'd Halls and broad Suburbean Park,

> To come the daily dull official round;
>> And home again at night with my pipe all alight,
>>> A-scheming how to count ten bob a pound. (63)

Deprived of light and air, this urban dweller is carried without purpose on his daily route. The sense of victimization grows as he gives us the details of his suburban home:

> And it's often very cold and very wet,
>> And my missis stitches towels for a hunks;
> And the Pillar'd Halls is half of it to let —
>> Three rooms about the size of travelling trunks.
> And we cough, my wife and I, to dislocate a sigh,
>> When the noisy little kids are in their bunks.

Under the restraint of small rooms, underground trains, and the repression of sighs is a 'god-almighty devil singing small' who would 'like to squelch the passers by against the wall'. The struggle appears in his use of language. Self-conscious about his choice of words, metaphors, or allusions, the clerk is discovering a luxuriant, vital language to portray his 'daily dull official round'. He stops himself: 'That's rough a bit and needs its meaning curled', or 'I've got to cut my meaning rather fine'. Nevertheless, the extravagance of such metaphors as the good and bad angels, reinvented in a modern and comic form as those who 'ride me like a double-seated bike', outdo the ironically named Mr. Silver-tongue. The sheer vitality of the clerk's search for phrases raises the music-hall song and diction to the level of dramatic poetry.

As the evidence describing the clerk's straits builds up, the anger turns against his auditor. Anticipating Mr. Silver-tongue's objections, he rebuts:

> I ain't blaspheming, Mr. Silver-tongue;
>> I'm saying things a bit beyond your art:
> Of all the rummy starts you ever sprung,

Thirty bob a week's the rummiest start!
With your science and your books and your the'ries
    about spooks,
    Did you ever hear of looking in your heart?

He then adds, 'I didn't mean your pocket, Mr., no'
(64). In this struggle the search for a significant
language and interpretation of life begins: 'If it doesn't
make you drink, by Heaven! it makes you think,/ And
notice curious items about life'. The poem shifts here
from aggression towards Mr. Silver-tongue to an
exploration of those qualities from within that give the
clerk 'The bally power to be bossed'. When the clerk
shifts to a formulation of his personal philosophy,
Davidson shifts but sustains the characterization. There
is a sense that the formulation has taken place prior to
the poem, as he introduces his ideas: 'And it's this way
that I make it out to be'. Yet the struggle that has
taken place earlier in the poem continues in the clerk's
attempt to find the exact words for his thoughts. The
questions, exclamations, curses, and improvisation that
have conveyed the drama of his struggle so far are
reduced, but they do not disappear.

He concludes with a series of analogies piled one on
top of another. The effect is of a struggle to find the
right metaphor, or with each new analogy to add to
the burden already imagined:

It's a naked child against a hungry wolf;
    It's playing bowls upon a splitting wreck;
It's walking on a string across a gulf
    With millstones fore-and-aft about your neck;
But the thing is daily done by many and many a one;
    And we fall, face forward, fighting, on the deck.

                                                    (65)

They are clichés, but it is appropriate that this most
vigorous characteristic of the clerk's language should

here multiply in an attempt to grasp and retain his idea. Throughout, the clerk fails to define his experience explicitly: he grasps for similes, for what the situation is *like* rather than what it *is*. Nevertheless, the truth is in the struggle. He reveals himself in his struggle and failure with language: this is his situation. Neither the natural man nor the philosophic man, he flounders ('fall[s], face forward, fighting') in a world of imitation and repression.

'Thirty Bob a Week' stands as an expression of these conditions and, as such, Davidson has made this mundane clerk moving. He has bridged the gap, has connected the prose and the passion, through the passionate poetry of a bookkeeper.[7] The prosaic suburban clerk has reached through his anger to a passionate understanding of his world and his condition. The poem succeeds because the sympathy is always with the clerk who, although he 'couldn't touch a stop and turn a screw', is raised to a heroic level through the dignity and the power of his struggle. Whether or not we accept the clerk's philosophy, which foreshadows Davidson's later scientific materialism, the poem is still successful. Unlike some of his testaments and tragedies where, as Virginia Woolf said, 'if you do not agree with him you are damned',[8] Davidson's 'Thirty Bob a Week' excels in the presentation of a character made vivid through dramatic detail and idiomatic language.

The poem not only succeeds in portraying realistically the emotional experience of an emerging class, but also succeeds in conveying Davidson's own personal struggles. The Cockney clerk was an appropriate vehicle for him, since the financial concerns and particular economic position of the clerk, as well as those of the music-hall artiste, were analogous to his own: having to make a go of it on thirty bob a week and 'think that that's the proper thing for you'.

Davidson too had to contend with the ride to suburbia, the cramped terraced row housing, and not much more than thirty bob a week. Even at the height of his success, he evidently never made more than £100 a year from his writing.

In a few later poems, Davidson adapts the monologue for collective voices in comparable, if not identical, economic situations. In 'Piper, Play', the sympathy is with the haggard factory workers released from work:

Now the furnaces are out,
    And the aching anvils sleep;
Down the road the grimy rout
    Tramples homeward twenty deep.
        Piper, play! Piper, play!
            Though we be o'erlaboured men,
        Ripe for rest, pipe your best!
            Let us foot it once again!

Bridled looms delay their din;
    All the humming wheels are spent;
Busy spindles cease to spin;
    Warp and woof must rest content.
        Piper, play! Piper, play!
            For a little we are free!
        Foot it girls and shake your curls,
            Haggard creatures though we be! (102–3)

In 'Waiting', Davidson portrays the unemployed as victims of the irresponsible wealthy, but proceeds to call on the wealthy for conscientious action, that is, for leadership. So the poor willingly relinquish what power they might have, 'waiting' to be led to work and ultimately to imperialist exploitation of other countries, for 'lands await our toil/ And earth half empty rolls' (119).

Critics are at variance in assessing the jingoist sentiments in Davidson's poetry. Some have argued that Davidson gives in to the worst kind of imperialist ranting, all in the name of heroic vitalism and the superiority of the British race. No one can deny the simplistic jingoism of 'Ode on the Coronation of Edward VII, of Britain, and of Greater Britain, King' and 'Song for the Twenty-Fourth of May', but a critic such as Northey has argued that these 'coincided with a time of personal and national crisis', and that 'Davidson's flirtation with imperialism was not truly integral to his whole outlook'.[9] A poem such as 'Coming' must be seen in its context, which was a series of poems that dramatically tried on various masks, one of them being that of the jingoist. The poem calls for armed intervention in the middle east, but alone the references to God signal Davidson's own distance from the material.[10]

Jingoism was one of the less attractive features of the music-hall song in its day. In many ways, 'Thirty Bob a Week' seems to give in to other palliatives of the popular entertainment form, making sentimental references to marriage and relinquishing class action for individual self-reliance. But, in fact, at each point when the clerk might give in to easy sentiment, the poem shifts to real anger and real passion. In a slightly different manner, 'War-Song', a poem often taken to be proof of Davidson's call for imperial violence, combines sympathy for the soldier and a realist's assessment of war.

In the voice of the soldiers, the poem strips away all illusions about the sanctity of war. These soldiers not only admit to ravaging lands and murdering people, but to a lust for blood that is inevitably aroused by murder. 'War breeds war again', and ties us to perpetual murder and devastation:

We thirty million trained
    And licensed murderers,

Like zanies rigged, and chained
    By drill and scourge and curse
In shackles of despair
    We know not how to break —
What do we victims care
    For art, what interest take
In things unseen, unheard?
    Some diplomat no doubt
Will launch a heedless word,
    And lurking war leap out!

We spell-bound armies then,
    Huge brutes in dumb distress,
Machines compact of men
    Who once had consciences,
Must trample harvests down —
    Vineyard, and corn and oil;
Dismantle town by town,
    Hamlet and homestead spoil
On each appointed path,
    Till lust of havoc light
A blood-red blaze of wrath
    In every frenzied sight. (128)

When we arrive at the last lines — 'Wherefore we now
uplift/ Our new unhallowed song:/ The race is to the
swift,/ The battle to the strong' — we have enough
information from the preceding lines to see that this is
not so much a call for imperial action, as it is a realist's
statement of fact. The poem moves beyond any
humanist concerns, to state simply things as they are.

Davidson's monologues and songs inevitably faced
the realities of his time, searching out the truths that
had lain hidden. As John Herdman has remarked:
'Endowed with a strong and subtle intellect and
considerable psychological penetration, Davidson drove
many of the commonplaces of late Victorian and
Edwardian thought and attitude to their logical,

unpalatable, but usually unexpressed conclusions'.[11] The 'personations' in the monologues allowed Davidson to move into the voices of figures who were caught in a certain economic situation and, in the best poems, to explain that situation from within. At times the music-hall genre allowed him to get away with caricature, but in his best monologues the character and the situation are explored in depth. In the eclogues Davidson would try another economic group — Fleet Street journalists and would-be poets in London in the nineties.

NOTES

1. W. B. Yeats, 'The Celt in London. The Rhymers' Club', *Boston Pilot*, 23 April 1892; rpt. in *Letters to the New Island*, ed. Horace Reynolds, Cambridge, Mass. 1970, p. 144.
2. W. G. Blaikie Murdoch, *The Renaissance of the Nineties*, London 1911, p. 22.
3. Yeats, p. 144.
4. Yeats, p. 145.
5. *Yellow Book*, 2 (1894), 99.
6. See G. L. Anderson, 'A Social Economy of Late Victorian Clerks', in *The Lower Middle Class in Britain 1870–1914*, ed. Geoffrey Crossick, London 1977, pp. 131-2.
7. Comparisons can be made with E. M. Forster's Leonard Bast in *Howards End* (1910), London 1973, p. 113.
8. Virginia Woolf, 'John Davidson', *TLS*, 16 August 1917, p. 390.
9. Northey, p. 10.
10. Northey, p. 10.
11. 'John Davidson in Full', *Akros*, 9 (1974), 82.

CHAPTER 4

THE ECLOGUES

> When I was a teacher in Scotland, I had the idea of writing a kind of teacher's calendar on the plan of the old Shepherd's Calendar, but this idea was never carried out. When my father died, however, among the books that came into my possession was a copy of Gibbon's *Decline and Fall*. As I read it the old idea revived, but I was in London now, and the journalists of Fleet-street seemed closer friends than the teachers of my young days. So I wrote a journalist's calendar, under the title of *Fleet-street Eclogues*, and every morning, before sitting down to my desk, I read a chapter of Gibbon.[1]

Davidson's choice of the pastoral eclogue and Shepherd's Calendar to document the decline and fall of his London world coincides with other archaic and conservative tendencies in his work and confirms his title of modern Elizabethan poet.[2] But the incipient irony of the title suggests a parodic inversion that shifts the centre of this traditionally pastoral genre from the country to the city.

In all, Davidson published twenty-eight eclogues, twenty-four of them forming two complete calendar cycles. The first cycle began with the seven poems in *Fleet Street Eclogues* (1893) and was completed in *A Second Series of Fleet Street Eclogues* (1896). In March 1905 Davidson began a new calendar cycle, publishing one a month in the *Outlook* for ten months. As if to set all in order, he completed this cycle just before his death. A January eclogue was printed in the *Westminster Gazette* on 13 February 1909, and a February eclogue was left in the manuscript of *Fleet Street and Other Poems* when Davidson disappeared.

The dramatic voices of his literary journalists may have been modelled on specific friends — Le Gallienne, Yeats, William Watson, Quiller-Couch, or Wemyss Reid — but they are probably 'a composite self-portrait',[3] with Menzies and Brian as the pessimists, complaining of their contemporary urban life; Basil as the Romantic, yearning for the regenerative beauty of nature; Sandy as optimist and activist; and Percy as the tempered old wise man. The irony of the Fleet Street context is made explicit when one journalist is chided by his colleagues for masquerading as a simple and natural man:

Brian: I love not brilliance; give me words
        Of meadow-growth and garden plot,
        Of larks and blackcaps; gaudy birds,
        Gay flowers and jewels like me not.

Basil: The age-end journalist it seems
        Can change his spots and turn his dress,
        For you are he whose copy teems
        With paradox and preciousness. (203)

The pastoral tradition is ironically laid to rest. In the very act of adopting the eclogue genre, Davidson implies it is no longer viable in the modern world. The paradox of *Fleet Street Eclogues* is in this self-awareness. The modern poet is no longer able to masquerade as shepherd or swain, even though he may yearn to do so. Davidson's eclogues explore the implications of the pastoral from the new perspective from within the city, that is, at the very centre of the city's production of words, of news and stories, of truth and lies: Fleet Street. The entire pastoral genre must be re-evaluated in the light of the modern urban experience, in the light of what Arthur Symons was later to call 'the test of poetry which professes to be modern', that is, 'its capacity for dealing with London'.[4]

This *tour de force* of mock-pastoral succeeds because Davidson's concerns are with both the fallen world of the city and the ideal world of nature. One of the main narrative structures in these eclogues is the journalist's excursion out from the city's centre into the reviving world of the forest or field and his return to Fleet Street bearing the 'secret truths' of nature. Davidson's Utopian world is always that of the conventional genre in which 'the characters understand life in the relation not to man's activity but to the fundamental patterns of the created world: day and night, the seasons, birth and death, love and fear, fertility and drought'.[5] The overall structure of a calendar cycle allows him to explore the question of 'Time's hearse', of degeneration and progress, of accepting the natural cycle or transcending it.

Ultimately, Davidson's goal is to hold all contraries, including both worlds of the city and the country, in an ironic balance. 'Irony affirms and delights in the whole'.[6] This inclusiveness is achieved in the first cycle of *Fleet Street Eclogues*, but by 1905, when the second series is begun, Davidson's views have changed. The single voice of scientific materialism dominates any dialogue that is started. The eclogue form undergoes radical changes to suit that purpose.

First Cycle

The structure of these poems is based on an ironic interplay of multiple voices. In one poem, 'Lammas', this interplay is raised to a thematic level. Four journalists are not long into some praises of summer when dissension sets in:

Ninian: A truce to this!

Let us see things and say them. Why debate?

To this Sandy replies:

The blare of personal and party aims
In parliaments and journals seems indeed
No substitute for Sinai; but it serves:
And from the vehement logomachy
Of interest and cabal, something humane
At happy intervals proceeds.

Ninian's response is:

I see no hope in wrangling. Nations pass
From panic into panic; all men seem
Fools or fanatics. (237–8)

The poem speaks about itself, acknowledging the fallen world within which it exists. The visionary poem is not viable; the single prophetic voice is unavailable. The alternative here is debate, or at least a convening of opinions and of tales. The poem 'Lammas' actually moves into Ninian's world of 'Let us see things and tell', narrating his own story of personal anguish. Yet the resolution of the poem comes from the interplay of this and the advice of the other journalists.

The form of the interplay is not always that of debate. Its complexity is more akin to musical forms, to madrigal, fugue, or variations on a theme, as the case may be. The resolution is often found through tonal structure and imagery rather than through argument. For instance, in 'New Year's Day', the main structure is constituted by a debate on journalism, 'This trade that we ply with our pen,/ Unworthy of heroes or men' (194). It is linked to the beginning of a new year and to the themes of progress and degeneration. While some characters argue that 'Beauty and truth are dead,/ And the end of the world begun', and others that 'the future of the world is shaped by journalists', a third lyric voice (Basil's) is heard from the beginning in counterpoint to, but independent of, the discursive argument. Even when referring to the city, this journalist's tone is detached and, with its gentle rhythm, almost hypnotic: 'From the muted tread of the feet,/ And the slackening wheels, I know/ The air is hung with snow,/ And carpeted the street'. In opposition to Brian's age-end wintry world, Basil's lyric voice offers imagery of spring, evoking the eternal paradox of the imminence of one season in the other: 'Through the opening gate of the year/ Sunbeam and snowdrops appear'. Basil's speeches move independently towards their own climax of song and at that moment the debate is resolved. The journalists are all united in a communal drinking song in celebration of the new year and of journalism. Structurally, the poem advances towards its resolution much as the volume of *Fleet Street Eclogues* does as a whole. The discordant world of the city is evoked and examined while the world of the natural, of the ideal, and of the rural is presented alongside. The resolution never loses sight of either world. The echoes of discord or of harmony persist so that Davidson's ironic view of the universe is maintained. And though a tentative resolution may be reached within one poem, the volume as a whole illustrates the continued paradox.

The language of other poems also enacts this juxtaposition of contraries. A strong patina of Elizabethan diction, syntax, and dramatic repartee finds itself next to contemporary clichés or ninetyish purple patches:

Percy:

A-moping always, journalist? For shame!
Though this be Lent no journalist need mope:
   The blazing Candlemas was foul and wet;
   We shall be happy yet:
Sweethearts and crocuses together ope.

Menzies:

Assail, console me not in jest or trope:
Give me your golden silence; or if speech
    Must wake a ripple on the stagnant gloom
    Of this lamp-darkened room,
Speak blasphemy, and let the mandrake screech.

. . . .

Menzies:

And brooding thus on my ephemeral flowers
    That smoulder in the wilderness, I thought,
    By envy sore distraught,
Of amaranths that burn in lordly bowers,
Of men divinely blessed with leisured hours. ...

(198–9)

Other variations of the interplay occur in 'Queen
Elizabeth's Day' where all the characters make the
transition together from prosaic to poetic language, or
from one genre to another, as the topic of discussion is
altered. Thus the poem moves smoothly from urban
impressionism to rural description, and finally to
historical and metaphysical speculations. The opening
lines of 'St. George's Day' show how Davidson might
maintain the rhythm from one voice to the next, but
ironically introduce a radical shift in perspective:

Herbert:

I hear the lark and linnet sing;
I hear the whitethroat's alto ring.

Menzies:

I hear the idle workman sigh;
I hear his hungry children cry.   (222)

In 'Mayday', Menzies' ballad of the 'Martyr of romance', Basil's song of the nightingale and his carol, all celebrate in their different forms the theme of a lost age where May Day, with its romance, ritual, and communion with nature, was possible. With the mixture of genres here, the relationship between the different voices can still be described as musical in form, but it is a case of variations on a theme rather than of counterpoint or madrigal. Similarly, in 'Midsummer Day', Basil's memory of a scene by an Essex bridge and Sandy's of love and the scent of a rose are variations on the theme of nature's gifts. They are the 'rustic visions' that make us 'forget the wilderness/ Of sooty brick, the dusty smell,/ The jangle of the printing-press' (234).

The resolution implied in the successful eclogues is always the paradoxical irony that all contraries must and do co-exist. This resolution, implied through structure and imagery in 'New Year's Day' and other poems, is made philosophically explicit in Percy's tale of the old journalist in 'St. Valentine's Eve'. In answer to Menzies' intense struggle with 'life's question' and the limitations of human nature, Percy's mentor explains evil as the necessary complement to love:

If one man and one woman, heart and brain
    Entranced above all fear, above all doubt
    Might wring their essence out,
The groaning of a universe in pain
Were as an undersong in Love's refrain. (201)

When Percy suggests a rural escape as an antidote to Menzies' ennui, his evocation of a February rural scene is not without its own contraries:

And scent the spicy smoke
Of withered weeds that burn where gardens be;
And in a ditch perhaps a primrose see. (202)

And despite the lyrical, almost mediaeval, emblem of

February, the poem will not close without a reminder of that present world of discord. The harmonious emblem:

> From windy heavens the climbing sun shall shine,
>> And February greet you like a maid
>> In russet-cloak arrayed;
> And you shall take her for your mistress fine,
> And pluck a crocus for her valentine (202)

is balanced by: 'I shall see earth and be glad:/ London's a darksome cell where men go mad.'

Thus the main themes of pastoral are explored in Davidson's poems. Menzies' complaint against daily toil, which expands to include all physical, social, and economic factors controlling his life, is a dramatic expression of man's frustration with the limitations of the human condition within a 'fallen' world. The city is for the most part the core and symbol of this fallen world, a place of tumult and strife, of harried daily toil, dirt, and degeneration. Man is trapped even within the calendar itself. The inhabitants of the city of Dis are stifled by dog-day summers ('St. Swithin's Day'), and choked by October fog ('Queen Elizabeth's Day'). The journalists are concerned with their own over-worked condition or the unemployment on the street. Menzies complains of his youth spent in 'uncouth nauseous vennels, smokey skies' (200). In 'St. Swithin's Day', the 'devil's din' emanates from the city. The catalogue of ugly urban sounds is set up in contrast to the harmony of Basil's singing birds, which opened the eclogue. The fallen world, the world in time, the world of night, the world of Fate, are all in opposition to 'that green-crowned, sun-fronting mountain-brow' from which glimpses of infinity are possible. The complaint is against the human condition which makes us at the same time finite and desirous of the infinite. It is also against the man-made world, gathered emblematically

here in the city's cacophony that prevents and defeats
our 'aspirations':

> The clash of iron, and the clink of gold;
> The quack's, the beggar's whining manifold;
> The harlot's whisper, tempting men to sin;
> The voice of priests who damn each other's missions;
> The babel-tongues of foolish politicians,
> Who shout around a swaying Government;
> The groans of beasts of burden, mostly men,
> Who toil to please a thankless upper ten;
> The knowledge-monger's cry, 'A brand-new fact!'
> The dog's hushed howl from whom the fact was rent;
> The still-voice 'Culture'; and the slogan 'Act'!
> Save us from madness; keep us night and day,
> Sweet powers of righteousness to whom we pray.

(208)

The invocation to the 'powers of righteousness', the
litany of evils with an attempt to evoke some power
over them, and the extreme supplication are made
ironic by the sardonic tone. This cry against the
discrepancy between awareness and power, in
Davidson's terms between Righteousness and Fate, is
sent out 'Here from the city's centre... Where hawkers
cry, where roar the cab and bus'. But the ironic tone
signifies the opposite of a supplicating prayer. There are
no powers of righteousness and none who can protect
us. The poem is a complaint, but, like the clerk in
'Thirty Bob a Week', this journalist implies that no
power outside himself can change the way things are.

Linked to the city is the alienated labour that men
are bound to once they arrive in London. In 'New
Year's Day', Davidson suggests that the ideal world of
'ambition and passion and power' is not only distant in
time but also distant in space. London and
contemporary Fleet Street destroy the best in men who
arrive innocent from the provinces:

> Ambition, and passion, and power
> Come out of the north and the west,
> Every year, every day, every hour,
> Into Fleet Street to fashion their best:
> They would shape what is noble and wise;
> They must live by a traffic in lies. (194)

The journalists lament the debased world in which they live, comparing their newspapers' likes and literary pettiness to golden ages of the past, such as the time of Shakespeare and Elizabeth I in 'Queen Elizabeth's Day'. Action is reduced to a circling motion of degeneration: to meaningless repetitions — 'the life my echoing years repeat' (199); to stasis and stagnation — 'To me Time seems a dungeon vast/ Where Life lies rotting in the straw' (225); or alternatively to paralysis — 'I cannot act. The subtle coils grow tense,/ And crush my limbs, my heart, my throat, my head' (242). But the eclogues are notable for their contrasts, and their description of nature, the 'songs of the beauty of the country and the joys of life'[7] made at least the first volume of *Fleet Street Eclogues* 'perhaps the most memorable volume of the year [1893]'.[8]

The cry 'Has anyone been out of town?' or 'Who has been out of London?' invites the country into the journalist's office in Fleet Street, and when that occurs the monstrous city temporarily dissolves: 'The city with its thousand years,/ Like some embodied mood of mine/ Uncouth, prodigious, disappears' (234). From this vantage point, 'Heaven is to tread unpaven ground' and any glimpse of that rural world is a gratuitous 'foretaste... of Paradise'. Set in the heart of London, the poems in the voice of one or more characters often move out to the country and back again to Fleet Street. Davidson establishes the basic paradigm early in the series, where journalists return from another world (of nature usually, but also of a historical past, a personal past, of vision, or even of fairies), bringing with them the memories, tales, truths, or visions of that ideal world. When Menzies complains, in 'St. George's Day, 'my city spleen/ Holds [me] in a fretting bond', it is rural remedies that Herbert prescribes. To move into the world where 'the old stile stands... Footworn, its bars with many hands/ Polished like ebony', and where the 'antique footpath winds about', connecting and intertwining the farms and towns and waters and downs, is to move into an integrated world of community, tradition, and generation. They escape into the country, or into personal pasts of youth or love, into a national past (Elizabethan England when the Maypole stood in the Strand), or at times into a visionary experience beyond space and time. The poems thus celebrate epiphanic moments that reveal nature's 'secret truths', but they always return to the actual, frustrated world of the journalists in London. *Fleet Street Eclogues* and *A Second Series of Fleet Street Eclogues* attempt to straddle both the ideal and real worlds. Davidson differs from his romantic predecessors, in these early poems, in his effort to circumscribe these epiphanic moments with the city and the material world, and in his insistence that the infinite can exist only within the material world. One goal, perhaps *the* goal, towards which the poems strive, is the experience of the timeless and the infinite within the confines, and because of the confines, of the clock-measured reality 'that is too much with us', that is, within the material world and within the city.

Davidson also recognizes that alienation is not only found in the city but can be experienced, as in 'Lammas', in the face of nature when man expects some spiritual revelation from it. To Ninian's statement, 'I am besieged by things that I have seen:/ Followed and watched by rivers; snared and held/ In labyrinthine woods and tangled meads' (240), Herbert replies, 'You went forth seeking God and found the world/ The sounds and sights that haunt, and help and please'. He adds the advice:

> Blame not yourself too much; admit no fear
> Of madness with the sunrise in your blood;
> And hold your own intelligence in awe
> As the most high: there is no other God —
> No God at all; yet God is in the womb —
> A living God, no mystic deity.

. . . .

> So let us think we are the tortured nerves
> Of Being in travail with a higher type.
> I know that I shall crumble back to dust,
> And cease for evermore from sense and thought,
> But this contents me well in my distress: —
> I, being human, touch the highest reach
> Attained by matter, and within me feel
> The motion of a loftier than I:
> Out of the beast came man; from man comes God.
>
> (245)

The last lines of the poem give us Ninian's final 'yes' and a litany of lush natural scenes which contrast with the agony and the haunting qualities of his earlier nightmare scenes. The visions which had presented themselves as spectres now become 'themselves' — images of his own strength and latent divinity. This poem is proof against any hard and fast argument that Davidson's later ideas are radically different from those in his early work. In all these early eclogues Davidson hints at the possibility of the kind of renewal found in the traditional pastoral genre, including this proto-materialist position in 'Lammas'. Yet the structure of the debating voices and the constant reference back to the present world of Fleet Street prohibit any easy solution. The effect is generally one of a sense of struggle.

The Second Cycle

It is clear that Davidson's return to his Fleet Street eclogue form in 1905 was, on one level, primarily a commercial enterprise. His many theatre ventures had failed; his materialist *Testaments* were not selling; so he set up a contract with the *Outlook* to produce a poem a month, returning to a form that had proved popular and lucrative in the nineties. The first poem, 'The Ides of March', self-consciously begins with a general reunion of the eighteen-nineties journalists, and the 'golden age' of the poem is now set in 1895 when the Fleet Street eclogues journalists were enjoying their hey-day. When Davidson published this poem in his *Holiday and Other Poems* he deleted the entire introductory narrative, implicitly acknowledging that it was a mere advertising gimmick. And yet these later eclogues are best understood in relation to the first set of eclogues, since Davidson is always conscious of them, as if it were time already to parody or 'transvalue' his own works and genres. 'St. Mark's Eve', with its Highbeach tower-gong and dream of elves, is reminiscent of 'Michaelmas', with the bells of St. Paul and Basil's vision. 'The Twenty-Fourth of May' returns to the imperialist theme found in 'St. George's Day', while 'Bartelmas', 'St. Mark's Eve', 'Holiday', and 'November' adopt the convention of the journalist's journey out of London, and his return with sights and sounds for the others, a pattern established in the earlier poems, 'Good Friday', St. Swithin's Day', 'Mayday', and 'Midsummer Day'. Certain questions raised in previous poems are now re-examined and answered. In 'Michaelmas' Basil asked, 'But can a brazier hold the sun,/ Or any cup an ocean?' To this Menzies replied, 'None'. In 'New Year's Eve' Clarence echoes back, 'There is a dish to hold the sea,/ A brazier to contain the sun. ... That minister of ministers,/ Imagination, gathers up/ The undiscovered Universe/

Like jewels in a jasper cup' (284). Whereas the conflicting voices in the earlier poem represent viable alternatives, those in the later eclogue are mere foils for the one true voice. Clarence is able to say at the end of 'New Year's Eve' that he is 'One who can tell/ That false is false and true is true,/ Alive or dead, in Heaven or Hell' (285). This exclusive resolution would have been impossible in the earlier series. Even if a journalist had taken this position, the poem as a whole would have undermined it, through debate or ironic juxtaposition.

Thus the structure and form set up in the earlier poems for intrinsic reasons are reduced to mere conventions for the later cycle. Dissenting voices, usually represented by Brian or Menzies in such poems as 'New Year's Day', 'St. Valentine's Eve', and particularly 'St. George's Day', reappear in 'The Twenty-Fourth of May', 'Baptist Tide', and 'The Feast of St. Martha'. In 'St. George's Day' Menzies had presented the pessimist's stance, a stance accepted as viable throughout the early poems:

> I cannot see the stars and flowers,
> Nor hear the lark's soprano ring,
> Because a ruddy darkness lowers
> For ever, and the tempests sing.
> I see the strong coerce the weak,
> And labour overwrought rebel.... (223)

In the later 'Twenty-Fourth of May' Brian rephrases this position:

> To me the amber studs
> Of the kingcups on the leas,
> And the fragrant hawthorn buds
> Are but the earth's disease;
> And the daisies in the grass
> A snowy leprosy. (268)

However, whereas Menzies' voice in the early poem had persisted through to the end and modulated both sides of the issue to find a resolution that embodies both good and evil, pessimism and optimism, in the final cry, 'we are the world's forlorn hope', 'The Twenty-Fourth of May' abandons Brian's voice halfway through the poem. There is a new abstraction and distance from the reality of the issues which allows Davidson to write so conclusively on his jingoist theme:

Basil: Our England would remain
        Wherever men are free.

Ninian: Embattled usage falls
        At the beating of our drums;
        All proud originals
        Have scope where England comes.

Vivian: As free as birds that sing
        And serenade the morn. (269–70)

The interaction of Davidson's multiple voices has changed. When discussion does take place the dissenting voices function now as foils rather than as viable alternatives. The 'ironic' perspective embodied in the conflicting voices of the earlier poems is now replaced by an authorial voice that has the answer. In Percy's terms, the validity of prophecy has been re-established, rendering debate superfluous. The eclogue is now used in a new way, with emphasis on the harmony of the various parts rather than on their distinctiveness, giving the effect of a dramatic chorus. 'The Ides of March' amasses, voice by voice, attributes of spring, creating a communal expression of the death of winter and the coming of spring, while in 'St. Mark's Eve' the confluence of voices comes through repetition.

The poem moves through a series of questions and answers, the latter nearly rephrasing the former.

This later volume, *Holiday and Other Poems*, is marked by an intensive use of rhyme which, perhaps above all other formal characteristics, contributes to the poems' sense of unity over diversity:

> I have been in the wildwood, sirs,
> In the snare of a sovran rhyme;
> Where blossoms and feathers and furs
> Grow rich as a dazzling rhyme —
> With stains of a fragrant rhyme;
> And the very spathes and spurs
> Are tuned to the deafening chime
> Of the larks and the courage that stirs
> In the heart of the vernal prime. (264)

The intricate rhyme scheme, the insistent rhythm, and the highly repetitive phrasing have created a complete and closed world. The wildwood has become a self-contained, artificial, and, in Davidson's term, 'decadent' world, since the 'snare of a sovran rhyme' that encloses the character Vivian also captures the reader.

'Bartlemas' is one of the more interesting attempts in the later poems to integrate a unity of vision and the eclogue form. Taking for the first time the traditional pastoral singing-match, Davidson brings together the 'din' of Bartholomew's Fair and the 'harvested silences' of an autumnal forest. Basil as judge introduces the contest between Lionel and Vivian:

> Then you of the Forest shall spin
> A tissue of rhythmical words —
> Of jewelled, diaphanous words;
> And he shall delight in the din
> Of Smithfield and Bartlemas Birds —
> In the venial, carnival sin
> Of Bartholomew's roystering Birds;

While I as a guerdon prepare
　　In our mazer of maple that held
The hydromel, quaffed at the Fair
　　And older than scriptural eld. (276–7)

The harmony of sounds is again celebrated as it was in
'St. Mark's Eve'. The cries in Lionel's street no longer
have the dissonance of the 'devil's din' in 'St. Swithin's
Day'. The contraries of life are subsumed, not into a
prayer to the powers of righteousness, but into a world
of harmonious rhyme. The commingling of sounds,
smells, and sights in the Forest ('the seraphim mingle
their song,/ With perfume entangle the light') is echoed
in a similar process at the Fair where 'rose on the air,/
With the odour of burning entwined,/ The breath of an
agonised prayer... braiding the wind/ With an incense,
nor holy, nor rare/ When they tortured the flesh and
the mind'. Similarly, the colour of the autumnal forest
floor 'through the lacquer, the mordant, and dye' is
echoed in the Smithfield's 'cressets that lacquer the
sky'. The singing-match is never officially judged, for
the two worlds become one. Basil intimates as much:
'Green leaves in the Forest; green sleeves —/ I
modulate Lionel's cry —/ At the Fair; in the Forest,
green leaves'. We end as we had begun in 'St. Mark's
Eve' — 'in the snare of a sovran rhyme'. Above all, we
leave with a delight in the 'tissue of rhythmical words'.

　　Some changes in Davidson's use of the form suggest
that the eclogue itself is basically unsuited to his later
thought. The most striking misapplication of an earlier
convention is found in 'Holiday: A Fleet Street
Eclogue'. The occasion of the poem is Herman's return
from a 'holiday', and, as in 'St. Swithin's Day', he is
asked by the other journalists to 'Rehearse/ All your
pregnant holiday./ Whipping streams, or turning verse
—/ How you spent it, Herman, say' (498). These
mundane questions are here absurdly followed by an
allegory of the progress of mankind told in mythic

language and imagery. A Promethean figure who has lived and died and risen again on three occasions is reduced to parody by the structural framework which surrounds him. When Davidson subtracts this framework for the poem's publication in *Holiday and Other Poems*, Herman's speech shifts into the realm of ballad-tale, which, given its associations with the supernatural and romance, is a more appropriate medium for the poem's content.

For similar reasons, Davidson also abandoned the eclogue framework of 'St. Andrew's Day: A Fleet Street Eclogue' for its second printing. Lionel's lines — 'I, from wandering in the Regent's Park/ As you'd wander in the wildwood, come' (499) — introduce a series of November scenes, both urban and rural. It soon becomes clear that the framework is irrelevant, that there is no dialogue and no need for multiple voices. 'November', as it appears in *Holiday* and, in essence, as it appeared in *Outlook*, is a descriptive poem. In a letter to Mrs. Grant Richards, his publisher of this period, Davidson belittles this later series of eclogues in general and the November poem in particular: 'I am in travail with a stupid poem which won't come. I write one a month for money. But when you have published my *Theatrocrat* and the world's eyes are opened I shall be able to do my own things only'.[9]

Thematically, Davidson's revision of 'Michaelmas' in 'New Year's Eve' points to the principal differences between the two series of eclogues. The midnight gong of St. Paul's sets the stage in both poems. The imagery used to describe the sound in 'New Year's Eve' suggests, as elsewhere in this later volume, the harmony and order of Time: 'Each vibrant thought,/ An orb of music, fills the ear/ With rich harmonics interwrought' (283). Cyril reiterates the image of an ordered universe speeding through the galaxies and time:

The world speeds in a trance profound

> From dark abyss to dark abyss
> Across this twelve-arched bridge of sound
> Between the two eternities. (283)

However, from Clarence's point of view this order is unconscious, and therefore unchangeable and deterministic. He offers a description of a purposeful life and purposeful action, solving the dilemmas expressed by Brian, Menzies, and Ninian in the earlier series of eclogues:

> I want some reason with my rhyme,
> A fateful purpose when I ride;
> I want to tame the steeds of Time,
> To harness and command the tide:
>
> I want a whip whose braided lash
> Can echo like the crack of doom;
> I want an iron mace to smash
> The world and give the peoples room. (285)

Imagination will make this revolution possible. The indefinable moment of change from year to year, from past to future, had left Basil, in 'Michaelmas', with a vision he could not contain. The poem had ended with dissatisfaction and desire, with the gap between vision and reality. In 'New Year's Eve', vision and reality are made into one, and past and future are lost in the 'eternal present Now' with man's imagination controlling the passage of time. Integration and harmony are not sought for in a future apocalyptic New Jerusalem or in an Arcadia or Eden of the past. Remaining within time and within the process of matter, the eternal moment can be achieved. The problem of space and time, of the limitations of the human condition, which the eclogues had treated since 1893, here finds a solution when man's consciousness, his imagination, is able to perceive vision in reality.

Written not long after *The Theatrocrat*, 'New Year's

Eve' echoes many of the themes and creeds presented in that play. It also looks forward to Mammon's words on the nature of time:

Time is not; never was: a juggling trick,
A very simple one, of three tossed balls,
The sun, the moon, the earth, to cheat our sense
With day and night and seasons of the year.
This is eternity: here once in space
The Universe is conscious in you and me.[10]

This solution to the problem of space and time is at the heart of Davidson's later thought as expressed in his testaments and tragedies, and to a certain extent it is a solution which negates the calendar form of the eclogues. Once the 'eternal present Now' becomes absolute, January and June are irrelevant. In the earlier cycle of poems the calendar form had emphasized the passage of time, the confines of nature, and the necessity of contraries. Without any single answer to these problems, the monthly poems offered occasions for speculation on the theme of time and nature. Some voices celebrated and delighted in the natural order of the cycle, such as Basil in 'New Year's Day'. Others complained bitterly of its bondage. Still other voices offered death as the only sure solution to the bondage of time. Ninian's only hope was poison in 'Lammas', while Menzies in 'All Hallow's Eve' pitied the immortal elves 'for they never can shun/ Time's tyrannous control' (247). In the 1905 poems, nature's cycle is no longer significant in terms of Davidson's later overview. For instance, in 'Our Day', Nelson's heroic act and fame obliterate all turbulations of climate and the passage of time. The opening lines of the poem, which describe London in October, remind the reader that this is a Fleet Street eclogue for the month, but they have little to do with the main body of the poem. Perhaps only in 'New Year's Eve' is the natural occasion raised to prime thematic importance, and then only to question the validity of the calendar's cycle.

Davidson's original conception of a journalist's calendar modelled after the old Shepherd's Calendar no longer inspires these later works. The year's inevitable cycle has lost its urgency for the poet, just as the multiple voices no longer serve as necessary spokesmen for the viable alternatives in his ironic vision. Also, Davidson is no longer at the centre of the activities and society of Fleet Street, the spirit of which is lacking in the later poems. In conclusion, the eclogue form was uniquely suitable to Davidson's nineties thought: his use of the multiple voices was innovative and modern, and the pastoral calendar provided the appropriate framework for his central themes of man's relationship to time and nature. By 1905 Davidson's materialist concerns reinforced the earlier emphasis on this tie with nature, but in contrast, accentuated unity rather than diversity, singleness of vision rather than an ongoing debate. He turned finally to testament and tragedy to embody these materialist concerns.

NOTES

1. Quoted in Jane T. Stoddart, 'An Interview with Mr. John Davidson', *Bookman* (New York), 1 (1895), 86.

2. [Richard Le Gallienne], 'Logroller's Literary Notes of the Week', *Star* (London), 4 May 1893, p. 2.

3. Townsend, p. 206.

4. Arthur Symons, 'Modernity in Verse', *The Collected Works*, 9 vols., London 1924, VIII, 46.

5. Eleanor Terry Lincoln, Intro., *Pastoral and Romance: Modern Essays in Criticism*, Englewood Cliffs, N.J. 1969, pp. 2-3.

6. *MF*, p. 135.

7. H. J. C. Grierson, *Lyrical Poetry from Blake to Hardy*, London 1928, p. 140.

8. George Cotterell, '*Fleet Street Eclogues*', *Academy*, 44 (1893), 25.

9. Letter to Mrs. E. Grant Richards, 25 October 1905, P.U.L.

10. *TM*, pp. 143-4.

CHAPTER 5

THE TESTAMENTS AND TRAGEDIES

'The Testament of a Vivisector', the first of a series of poems which I propose publishing at intervals in this form, will hardly recommend itself to Vivisector or Anti-Vivisector; and the new statement of Materialism which it contains is likely to offend both the religious and the irreligious mind. This poem, therefore, and its successors, my 'Testaments', are addressed to those who are willing to place all ideas in the crucible, and who are not afraid to fathom what is subconscious in themselves and others.

John Davidson[1]

Davidson's testaments, written between 1900 and 1909, are long philosophical blank-verse poems, ranging in length from about 200 to 2000 lines. The subject matter of the poems includes torture, rape, and murder, as well as disquisitions on the evolution of man and the nature of ether. They are, with his three late tragedies, *The Theatrocrat*, *The Triumph of Mammon*, and *Mammon and His Message*, as Davidson says here, his 'new statement of Materialism' reaching to what he felt was subconscious in man and matter.

This scientific materialism, based on the nebular hypothesis and theories of the atomization of forces, on the writings of Ernst Haeckle and others, has little of scientific value today. It is interesting rather because it points out the basic structures of his later work. The drive to formulate a coherent world system stems from his own loss of God and his reluctance to accept the void that was left: 'We fill the abyss, left in the Universe/ By cancelling God, with the Universe itself./ Great it is, Gervase; but the terror of it!'.[2]

For a short while Davidson was content to fill up the void with paradox, or what he called 'irony', to accept all contradictions, and the multiplicity of the eclogues of the nineties conveys these paradoxical contradictions, but ultimately Davidson turned to phenomena themselves, to *matter* as truth — the sole substance and essence of man. There is no moral order to this 'mutable cosmos'.[3] The absurdities and injustices of Fate do not produce a President of the Immortals, as in Hardy, but only an unconscious a-moral energy. Man's salvation, writes Davidson, is not to hope that man's humanism might change the gods, but that matter's energy might, as he says, become felt and conscious in man. There is a great deal of Nietzschean freedom from the constraints of a Judeo–Christian ethos in Davidson. He sets aside liberal humanism to discover the energy and power, the truth beyond good and evil, that is matter. And here Davidson breaks with the Victorians and their emphasis on 'human qualities'.[4] Above all he wanted to establish the identity of man and nature and to show that the concept of humanity was an alien construct, a fiction: 'Man is inhuman. Humanity is as fanciful an ideal as divinity'.[5]

The description Davidson gives of the origins of the universe and the nature of matter in the prefaces and epilogues of his late testaments and tragedies is in terms of a movement between flux, instability and tension on the one hand, and contraction, formation, and stability on the other. 'This eternal tide of Matter, this restless ebb and flow, I call Immorality'.[6] The same movement appears in Davidson's poetry and thought: between flux and control, between a surrender to experience and a desire to reshape that experience in the mind, that is, to

recontain it within some system. In his politics it is
present in the opposition between his sympathy with
workers and the poor, and his proto-fascist desire to
eliminate problems by annihilation or by absolute
control. He attacks all systems, theories, and
abstractions, yet constructs his own system with which
to explain the universe. Within the system itself there is
an abandonment of the ego to the freely-flowing forces
of nature and subsequently a strengthening of the ego
in the knowledge of self-consciousness. From his
materialist position he conducts his own ideological
analysis of Christian myths and morality, showing up
the false consciousness of metaphysics and religion. But
then his own materialist position is itself ideological:
absolute and Utopian. His theorizing and his message
attempt to rewrite individual experience and history in
terms of a system, an activity highly suspect even by
the standards of his own principles.

   Davidson wanted to destroy the old fictions that held
men captive, be it sexually or economically. In their
place he offered a world of physical matter and force
that is not held by any morality or, he would have it,
ideology. One exists, one is material, and one thinks.
He put these truths together and came up with the
narrative of material evolution that culminates in man's
consciousness. Man is matter becoming self-conscious —
no more, no less. One is not born trailing clouds of
glory from a spiritual other world, but with a memory
of material forces, that is, the ebb and flow, the
contraction and release of the physical world. All one's
actions are explained in terms of these determining
forces. And one's freedom from any sense of
determinism comes from accepting one's role as a
sentient and rational being, or rather, in Davidson's
terms, as an imaginative being. Let your mind go and
it will take you through the history of the world ('Fleet
Street'). The ecstatic release momentarily resolves all

tensions, certainly all moral guilt and all economic and physical woe. The eternal here and now ironically takes you beyond the problems of an impoverished, sick poet living in a wet climate with little hope of people reading his poetry — to put it sceptically. To put it clinically, Davidson, like Freud's paranoid-schizophrenic, Dr. Schreber, felt the pulsations of the universe flowing through him. There was 'no distinction between man and nature'.[7] His schizophrenic side surrendered his personal voice to the voice of matter and in return became 'material of eternity, eternity itself, become conscious and self conscious'.[8] His paranoid side then returned to recontain the experience into a rational, inclusive system — and thus, the prefaces and epilogues of his later testaments and tragedies.

The Testaments

Beyond the fact that these poems are ostensibly dramatic monologues, it is difficult at first to identify one form to which they all adhere. The *Empire-Builder* and the *Prime Minister* include dream visions, while *The Testament of John Davidson* takes us through epic battles with gods and goddesses. What is a testament as a literary form? A last will and testament perhaps, the bequeathing of one's possessions, of all that one has acquired of value during one's life? Or is it simply a 'statement ... testifying to the fact, validity or worth of something'?[9] Davidson said, 'the spin of the penny determined whether I should call the poems statements or testaments',[10] and he insisted again and again that the new poetry was a statement of the world as it is: 'I am not preaching any gospel: who reads my Parable will see that I am trying to state The Nature of Things, beginning without any theory or system, but with my own experience and an acquaintance with such facts as

I have — both bases increasing as I go on'.[11] Are the poems rather Lucretian, offering Davidson's materialist view of the cosmos? Or is he preaching a gospel, despite his denials; on the one hand, throwing out all the old fictions, myths, and religions that speak only of a spiritual world rather than this one, and, on the other, setting up his own New Testament of beliefs? He later was to admit that he had a message and was trying to get it said.[12]

Literary models do exist, but the black humour, satire, and legal phraseology of Villon or the dramatic complaint of Henryson's *Testament of Cresseid* hardly come to mind while reading Davidson's poems. Although not all the characters in Davidson's testaments are on the point of death, they all look back over their lives and draw conclusions about their experience to pass on to some implied or specified auditor. Davidson's poems are in fact closest in form to the religious or political testament, in which an eminent person reviews his life, often returning to his mistakes (to warn his descendants), and often to a crucial moment of change and revelation.

In all, Davidson completed six so-called 'testaments': those of the Vivisector, the Man Forbid, the Empire-Builder, the Prime Minister, 'John Davidson', and a shorter satiric 'Testament of Sir Simon Simplex concerning Automobilism'. But 'Cain', a late poem that is not called a 'testament', is perhaps the truest testament in terms of its form.

It is remarkably close to a series of religious testaments called the *Apocryphal Testaments of the Twelve Patriarchs*, in which the twelve sons of Jacob one by one speak to their people about their past, about the lessons of their lives, and about a prophecy for the future. E. C. Perrow has described the basic formulae for these testaments: the testator '(1) explains who he is and what is his character, (2) confesses some sin' (or his freedom from some sin), '(3) warns against that sin, (4) prophesies that it will become a besetting sin among his posterity, and (5) comforts the despairing with a prophecy of Christ'.[13] The *Testament of Reuben* begins:

> When Reuben fell ill, his sons and his sons' sons were gathered together to visit him. And he said to them: My children, behold I am dying, and go the way of my fathers. And seeing there Judah, and Gad and Asher, his brethren, he said to them: Raise me up, that I may tell to my brethren and to my children what things I have hidden in my heart, for behold now at length I am passing away. And he arose and kissed them, and said unto them: Hear, my brethren, and do ye, my children, give ear to Reuben your father, in the commands which I give you.[14]

Davidson's Cain also addresses his descendants:

> My sons and daughters; children's children; Cain's Posterity:
>
> . . . .
>   I see them, — these
> The offspring of my loins: — Enoch and Irad,
> Sons and companions; generations; boys
> That promise to be great — Jabal and Jubal,
> And my namesake, Tubalcain.
>
> . . . .
> My blessing and God's curse be with you all.
> Lie down about me, stretched at length; behind
> There, sit or kneel; and let the standers ring
> Us closely round, that every one may hear.
> My children, I am dying. (449)

Remodelling this biblical scene in the light of Browning's or his own dramatic monologues, Davidson establishes Cain as a dramatic figure using techniques of psychological realism. He moves away from the biblical tone, introducing dramatic details through commands, exclamations, ellipsis, and implied dialogue. For instance, Cain forgets what he is about to say or addresses himself to a specific comment made by one of his followers ('... What? I bade them?'). Thus Davidson circumscribes the prophetic tone of Cain's message with the world of everyday life. After these brief preliminaries, Cain moves into a formal address to his tribe, stressing his old age, his experience, and his wisdom. Poised between imminent death and the experience of a long life, he speaks from a privileged position: the knowledge of both life and death will be the subject of the poem.

The dramatic monologue is structured so that the poem moves from Cain's prologue, or address to the Cainites, to his tale of Cain and Abel, and finally to prophecy. Within the tale he returns to one 'besetting sin' as did the Patriarchs in their testaments. The Cainites have already inherited God's curse through Cain; they now are about to inherit his understanding of that curse, of God, of sin, and of exile.

Davidson radically transforms the biblical story, making Cain into the gentle, loving older brother, and Abel ironically into a Byronic Cain: a frenzied, angry, sullen youth. The interpretation turns on the fact that Abel kills animals and Cain does not, a fact that has called up much exegesis in biblical studies. Davidson's Cain is the patient natural philosopher: 'I dug and planted; studied nature's way' (450). Abel, on the other hand, has Faust's inordinate demand for knowledge: 'It maddened him/ To watch how nature did, to know the thing/ Achieved and not to understand' (450–1). Again, like Byron's Cain, Abel looks towards the closed gates of paradise with longing and resentment: 'At times he gazed/ On Eden half a day in ecstasy;/ Or dark with sin hereditary, wrath/ And sorrow intermingled, frowned on heaven' (450). His anger at being excluded, his desire for knowledge and eternal life, destroy his own living, 'Until he fell down pulseless, breathless, dead/ It seemed' (450). Abel, rather than Cain, has inherited the curse of Adam: his hankering after the tree of knowledge and the tree of life.

When put to the test (and in Davidson's poem it is 'God's test' as much as Cain's and Abel's), God responds to the power of Abel's slaughter. Following Abel's logic, Cain deduces: if God accepted the blood of the bull, how much more will he prize Abel's. The older Cain looking back is still somewhat perplexed by God's actions: 'God preferred/ A bull's blood to my brother's: — still I think,/ Old, dying as I am, something went wrong/ In heaven' (455).

Nevertheless, it is Cain's poem, and the inconsistencies and oppositions within him communicate his struggle to comprehend his experience and his God. He invites his people to pray with him and then denounces his prayer as 'insolent'. His exhortations to his people are often qualified, with interjections implying a hope for a better world. Only one thing separates men: 'Our thoughts of God' (450). The poem ends with a hint of a different order, the 'Christian' Cain dramatically slipping back into his original character, seeing God as the loving lamb.

> Since in imagination we conceive
> A merciful, a gracious God of men,
> It may be that our prayer and innocent life
> Will shame Him into goodness in the end.
> Meantime His vengeance is upon us; so,
> My blessing and God's curse be with you all.   (456)

This may be Cain's way of prophesying, but any 'message' in this testament is necessarily framed by irony, a dramatic irony that allows the reader to identify with the tragedy of Cain's position and reduces the proseletizing spirit that otherwise mars Davidson's poems.

As dramatic monologues, the testaments offer the wisdom of the testator. Since these characters review their lives and search out significant moments and truths learned from these moments, they are comparable both to poets who, like Wordsworth, return and recollect, making sense of the past, and to writers of autobiography. Each testator is a poet trying to review his life, to apprehend and comprehend it, and ultimately to bequeath it. The Promethean task in 'Cain' and in all Davidson's testaments is to find meaning. Cain should do this by reverting to an ancient story which has held its 'meaning' through the ages. However, Davidson's modern spirit is present, on one level as he inverts conventional interpretation, displacing any easy traditional meaning, and on another with the irony of Cain's own stand, his fumbling with his interpretations, and his ambivalence towards God. Although the testament form implies a belief in the power of the mind to unify disparate activities of the past and to collect them in one mind, Davidson's poems, with the full consciousness of their author or not, subvert that belief.

Each testament will have both a statement of the world as the testator now knows it with an account of his original 'sin' and a prophecy about the future, and a counter movement that undermines that statement, or at least the certainty with which it is given. Thus the irony. Ritchie Robertson, in the latest study of Davidson's testaments, explains this doubleness in terms of the tension between the essential will of the universe acting within the speaker and the individual ego or empirical personality.[15]

In *The Testament of a Vivisector*, Davidson's first testament and the closest to Browning's psychological monologues, the Vivisector gives an account of his

discovery of the answer to the riddle of the Universe —
what is life and what is man. The discovery comes
through his experiments, in particular one in which he
tortured a dying horse for two days, prodding its
exposed spinal column. The torture of the old nag is at
the centre of the poem — it was, so to speak, the
Vivisector's virtuous action that counteracted the sinful
humanitarianism all around him. The besetting sin of
mankind is to be too human, to care for the individual
and happiness rather than for the race and painful
material knowledge. Only when we give in to the force
of matter, a force that provides only pain, will we earn
self-consciousness, the goal, if any, of the universe.

The Vivisector speaks his testament to his
contemporaries, with satiric jabs at their complacency:

> Appraise me! — you, Christian of any stock:
> Suave Catholic, whose haunting art avails,
> Though fires are damped and sophistry undone;
> Evangelist, with starved and barren brain,
> Preying on evil consciences; or you,
> Courageous Anglican, the well-beloved,
> Enfeoffed with freehold in the City of God,
> And happy here upon commuted tithes —
> Your vested interests snug and ancient lights. (324)

In the face of these and others, the Vivisector has
retreated into isolation. He 'frequents/ The labyrinthine
fires of solitude/ Wherein the thinker, parched and
charred, outlives/ Milleniums in a moment' (324). And
the knowledge gained by isolation and suffering he now
passes on to posterity.

The Testament of a Vivisector gives in fact a capsule of
Davidson's early formulation of his scientific monism.
Man is only material, a part of and a medium for the
force of matter that is 'craw[ing] and grop[ing]' toward
thought. Borrowing catechetical formulas, the
Vivisector claims: 'Chief end of man, the ultime design/

Of intellect, is knowledge undefiled/ With use or usufruct' (325). The path toward self-knowledge is pain. From inclement skies or antagonism in love to death itself, affliction forces us to know ourselves and our material essence. In the history of mankind man has rebelled against these afflictions, chiefly death, by creating the idea of God, heaven, and hell. The Vivisector's experience of pain, both his own and that of those he tortures, sends him back to nature to reinterpret all actions, all movement, as painful. He completes his testament with a combination of creed and prophecy:

> And I believe that they who delve the soil,
> Who reap the grain, who dig and smelt the ore,
> The girl who plucks a rose, the sweetest voice
> That thrills the air with sound, give Matter pain:
> Think you the sun is happy in his flames,
> Or that the cooling earth no anguish feels,
> Nor quails from her contraction? Rather say,
> The systems, constellations, galaxies
> That strew the ethereal waste are whirling there
> In agony unutterable. Pain?
> It may be Matter in itself is pain,
> Sweetened in sexual love that so mankind,
> The medium of Matter's consciousness,
> May never cease to know. (328–9)

Although he inflicts pain with not a little sadism, the pain returns to him. His torture of the horse is comparable to the poet's prying into his own and others' self-consciousness — both lead to the 'reservoir of pain' that is our essence. The Vivisector, like the poet, is driven and allows himself to be driven by the force of matter, that leads towards self-consciousness. What tension there is in the poem comes from the voice of the family man who has lost wife and daughters, the man who suffers nightmares from the memory of former

times, undermining the voice of the man who has found
material truth. He, like all the other testators, has not
yet fully purged himself of all his humanitarian
sentiments.

I do not have space here to deal with all the
Testaments at length. In general, what makes these
poems interesting is their iconoclasm and critique of the
contemporary world; their moments of strong poetry, at
times lyrical and even plaintive; and the dramatic
struggle I have been describing that goes on inside each
testator.

The Testament of an Empire-Builder begins with the
Empire-Builder bed-ridden, suffering tormenting
thoughts and dreams. The process of the poem takes
him from this state through a series of visions that are
symbolic representations of the anxieties expressed in
the opening scene. These dream visions include a
parliament of beasts who discuss evolution and the
nature of man, and a vision of heaven and hell. Finally,
the anxiety is relieved as his former life of action is
retrieved, reaffirmed, and bequeathed, but not without
acknowledging the brutality of imperialism:

> What! tenfold a criminal?
> No other name for Hastings, Clive, and me!
> I broke your slothful dream of folded wings,
> Of work achieved and empire circumscribed,
> Dispelled the treacherous flatteries of peace,
> And thrust upon you in your dull despite
> The one thing needful, half a continent
> Of habitable land! The English Hell
> For ever crowds upon the English Heaven.
> Secure your birthright; set the world at naught;
> Confront your fate; regard the naked deed.
> Enlarge your Hell; preserve it in repair;
> Only a splendid Hell keeps Heaven fair. (349)

And, as in the *Vivisector*, the speaker cannot bequeath his legacy without some inner conflict: 'For even in Heaven each ransomed soul frequents/ A private, an inevitable Hell!)' (348)

The ambivalence is even stronger in *The Testament of a Prime Minister*. He is dying, and dying in dread and doubt: 'I go despairing down/ To dust and deep oblivion' (349). The crack which appeared at the end of the *Empire-builder* is now an open fissure. The Prime Minister is 'Undone by mystery, smitten by a thought,/ A poisoned arrow from the infinite./ Or is it that my spirit slays itself?/ A doubter always, I' (349). He will journey through various dream-like scenes, as the Empire-Builder before him, to come to terms with his doubt and death. Again, the legacy is one of struggle.

The prologue which presents the Prime Minister's anxieties leads back to the moment of rupture. His tale begins ('When I was master of the world') with a debate in Parliament. At a moment of affirmation in a materialist world, the Prime Minister was struck with doubt. His journey from this moment of rupture takes him through the city and to a discussion among a group of tramps (the eclogue journalists have been replaced by 'Incompetent or drunken' vagabonds in the back eddies of the Thames). This discussion concludes with the story of a man who rapes, then marries, and finally kills a woman, and murders their children. The Prime Minister also witnesses an allegorical pageant, a 'gorgeous masque' of 'twenty centuries of Christendom' (367). The body becomes a time machine transporting the Prime Minister back in time to recapture events and their meaning. These and a vision of the Last Judgement bring him to 'material truth', or 'the pageant of Becoming' (371).

The poem ends with again a juxtaposition of affirmation and fear. With echoes of Hamlet's 'To be, or not to be', the sequence is one of Davidson's

strongest expressions of a tortured mind and an attempt
to master it:

... the conscious Matter which I am,
Beginning to surrender consciousness,
Recoils from dissolution and divorce.
To be dispersed in elemental sport
Of heedless energy — the uncontrolled
Imagination of the Universe,
That flashes out an instant nebula
By chance encounter in the spacious dark
Of ancient suns extinct and vagrant, turns
To teeming wonder every water-drop,
Afflicts the human race with hope, attunes
The nightingale, and launches in the deep
The monstrous rorqual: to be left once more
A scattered wreck of groping elements
Without remembrance, judgement, wisdom, choice,
Perturbs the divers stuff that men are of;
Wherefore when sleep in mimicry of death
Dissolves self-consciousness, the hideous dreams
That wake me shrieking ...

    Let them come again
When sleep rehearses death, or death itself
Takes up the cue: no dreams of mine are they,
But Matter's dreams of old experience wrought
In imperceptive atoms: while I wake
I apprehend and master time and space,
For this self-consciousness is masterdom.

                 (372; Davidson's ellipsis)

Davidson first referred to his last testament as 'The
Testament of a Deliverer', then as the 'Passionary of
John Davidson', and finally as *The Testament of John
Davidson*.[16] The poem follows the structure we have
seen so far: a man returns over his life to find his
significant achievements and to recount them for

posterity. The prophet's role is reinforced by the concept of a Deliverer, and the sense of the testament as significant biography is conveyed in the word 'passionary', 'an old almost unused word for the history of a passion — any passion: the passion of Christ or of Sappho'.[17] Within this basic structure, 'John Davidson' tells a legendary tale of his battle with classical and Christian fictions. The testament is transformed into an epic world of gods and chariots, dragons and ambrosia. After an initial 'statement' of his materialist theories the hero literally flies off into another world where Diana, Apollo, and Thor are the leading characters. 'John Davidson' follows an epic hero's path, does battle with a dragon, kills off the archaic father deities, drinks ambrosia, and seduces Diana. These last two acts call for remorse and punishment, since his appointed task is to expel these gods from consciousness, not to become one of them himself. At this point the poem incorporates a Christian model into the classical tales, and 'John Davidson' descends into hell to witness the death of the gods and also to endure his own crucifixion. Having suffered this passion, he can rise again and return to the earth and matter from which he came.

The use of myth in *The Testament of John Davidson*, as Douglas Bush has pointed out, controls Davidson's 'demonic energy' and clarifies 'his turbid imagination'.[18] The poem 'is the work of a real if ineffectual Titan'.[19] Because the reader is able to refer to the well-known classical context of the poem, the story line is clearest in this testament: 'The mythological passages are written with a force and splendour which set them apart from most tame poetry of the period'.[20] Nevertheless, since his aim is to demolish the world of past fictions, Davidson's poem, exploiting as it does the classical and Christian paradigms, is a highly ambitious work of parody. At each moment that the reader and 'John Davidson' become involved in this mythic world, Davidson must remind us that his aim is to put it all into question. Thus the splendid ironic battle with Diana's dragon is permeated with an air of fustian, with the 'archaic jangle of celestial spear'. Davidson's Hell of Deities is an extravaganza of physical torture, and, Bosch-like, it gives the evanescent, fictional gods their final materialist nemesis:

> Supine or prone
> The fairies, kobolds, dwarfs, by pins and nails
> Transfixed like butterflies and beetles, screamed
> With stretched mouths, wings a-buzz and wriggling
>   limbs;
> And though they wrenched and wrung their bodies,
>   — they,
> And every sufferer there, incessantly —
> The puncture of the impalement sucked the stake
> Like a fierce mouth, such was the energy
> Constrictive in the magic metal lodged. (423)

Davidson's greatest struggle here is to maintain the parody in the poem, a struggle in which he is not always successful. Having chosen the classical model, he risks defeating his own purpose — the parody is at times recontained in the original other-world perspective. At other times, such as the seduction of Diana, there is an embarrassing gap between fiction and reality. His hero falls into the trap of the other gods, and Davidson himself seems overcome by his model, so that fantasies of flying through the air and seducing goddesses are validated by the poem as much as, if not more than, the material experience of matter and nature.

Davidson originally insisted on the 'dramatic spirit' of these testaments, that he must not be confounded with his created personae. Nevertheless, with *The*

Testament of John Davidson ('which is my personal poem, which is me', he wrote to Grant Richards) Davidson created 'a legendary figure in [his] own name'.[21] In an early article on interviews, Davidson maintained that we need 'to lay bare, encounter, to say, as well as be, what we are — not what we imagine ourselves, not even what we would like to be'. At the same time, the best interview gives 'an ideal biography ... a legend — a splendid background'.[22] It seems that *The Testament of John Davidson* was an attempt to create an 'ideal biography'. He even included two other personal poems in the volume, one about his youth as Prologue ('Honeymoon'), and one about the end of his life as Epilogue ('The Last Journey'). The poem does offer Davidson's 'personal utterance on the Universe become conscious';[23] it also conveys the sense of exile, of striving, and of failure that are so much a part of Davidson's life. His ambition, like that of his personae, was to annihilate the old Christian world view, to dispel the gods and Christian morality, and to lead the world to an understanding of its true nature, which is material, not spiritual. The tale of 'John Davidson' is an adequate allegory of the poet's mind. The battle with the dragon and gods and the hell scene are plausible nightmare and fantasy worlds. One of 'John Davidson's' battles takes the form of a singing contest in which 'John Davidson' sings his song of man and the universe, of a greater glory that is man's. As he reduces Apollo to a mere projection of man, the god weakens and dissolves. Thus, at the core of the poem is this song of man, which is also Davidson's song.

Davidson attempts to create a new Romantic myth with 'John Davidson' as its hero or 'deliverer' destroying the old world and beginning the new. However, the task he has set himself is extremely precarious. We are faced with not merely a question of the validity of confessional poetry, or of the creation of a fully dramatic presentation. Davidson tries to keep his own person as the hero of an entirely fabulous tale, an attempt which could only succeed if the irony of the situation were sustained, and Davidson is not able to do this consistently. The first-person narration makes the reader ill at ease as this Clark Kent suddenly leaves his desk to do battle with the world of metaphysics.

Compared to Davidson's earlier masks and personae, the testators are not as developed in terms of character, individual speech, or the realism of their situations; nevertheless, the poems do maintain the sense of a mind wandering, fumbling, hesitating, and struggling, as we have seen. And this is one of the most subtle and important aspects of Davidson's testaments. The testators are figures in torment, and therefore the testament is not only a dictation of their life-long findings, but the actual struggle to find meaning, to come to terms with the events and implications of their lives.

One of the major issues in critical discussions of Davidson's poetry has been his use of blank verse. Some contemporary reviewers praised it as 'the best since Milton';[24] others found it outmoded and monotonous. The same difference of opinions persists in the second half of the twentieth century: Eliot called it 'hard-going', while Turnbull insists it is a successful attempt to embody Davidson's later thought.[25] Davidson's blank verse characteristically consists of difficult, compressed, run-on lines. There are often catalogues of phrases, objects, or arguments in apposition, with sentences continuing for forty lines, as in the opening lines of *The Testament of John Davidson*:

When suddenly the world was closed to me,
And every road against my passage barred,
I found a door that opened into space;
I built a lodge celestial for myself,
An outcast's palace in the Milky Way;

> I banqueted my body and my soul
> On light and sound, the substance of the stars,
> Ethereal tissue of eternity;
> And took my ease in heaven, the first of men
> To be and comprehend the Universe: —
> To know how all things are the infinite
> Imponderable ether that possessed
> Illimitable space with tension (pure
> Spontaneous energy, the pristine state
> Of matter and its last consummate doom)
> Before the galaxies with silver seamed
> The swart oblivion of the Universe,
> Or pearly nebula began to glow
> Upon the sable bosom of the night,
> Or any living nerve electric leapt
> To elemental ecstasy. (380)

Davidson begins the poem with a few lines of regular blank verse, all lines end-stopped and the syntax clear. But it is only an introduction. A shift in pace comes definitely and appropriately with the word 'infinite'. With the introduction of this concept, the lines, phrases, parentheses, and polysyllabic words all accumulate. The rhythm and the pace imitate the subject: the infinite ether filled with tension. Barring free verse, blank verse was the one form which could allow Davidson this liberty, and he exploited it to the full.

Turnbull has argued that 'Davidson, in the interest of flexibility, tends to eliminate from his blank verse what might be called "operatic" features of the traditional form — the formal, periodic structuring of the verse paragraph'.[26] This is truer of Davidson's last volume of poems, especially 'Crystal Palace', than it is of his testaments. The varying length of the paragraphs and the fluid transition from one to another often disguise the form, but the underlying structure of much of the blank verse in these poems is the verse paragraph.

The Testament of a Man Forbid has some of the best poetry of his testaments. Davidson is incidentally again in his walker's guise, observing the natural world, this time near Shoreham. The materialist dimension to his observations does not take away from the lyric quality of the poetry; it fits in here, without too much strain on the vocabulary and the tone:

> So I went forth for evermore forbid
> The company of men. The Universe,
> Systems and suns and all that breathes and is,
> Appeared at first in that dread solitude
> Only the momentary, insolent
> Irruption of a glittering fantasy
> Into the silent, empty Infinite.
> But eyes and ears were given to me again:
> With these a man may do; with these, endure.
> I haunt the hills that overlook the sea.
> Here in the Winter like a meshwork shroud
> The sifted snow reveals the perished land,
> And powders wisps of knotgrass dank and dead
> That trail like faded locks on mouldering skulls
> Unearthed from shallow burial. (333)

The ambition implicit in these testaments ranks Davidson with epic poets. The testament form, the language, and the verse do help to validate these new myths of the material universe. However, the fulfilment of this ambition to write a series of successful epic poems in blank verse may have been impossible at the turn of the century. The twentieth century has trained us all to listen to the understatement, to the hidden allusion, and the silences between the lines. Even Davidson was aware in 1892 of the problems surrounding the long poem.[27] Above all, Davidson's poems need a sense of irony, and, although it is present, his proselytizing spirit often intervened. Davidson faced similar problems with the tragedies written at this time and in the same spirit. Perhaps only his last volume of poems, *Fleet Street and Other Poems*, which is more successful at sustaining an ironic voice in its observations and critique of the world around him, appeals to the modern reader.

The Tragedies

Understated, the tragedies are not. Davidson's late plays, the ones he felt were so many years before their time, all attempt to overthrow the morality and consciousness of the Christian West. The plays supposedly take us first through a prologue to this revolution (*The Theatrocrat: A Tragic Play of Church and Stage*), then through the revolution itself (*The Triumph of Mammon*), and finally through the political implementation of its ideals (*Mammon and His Message*). In these last plays, Davidson's hero 'transcend[s] all dishonour, all crime, the utmost evil that he could do, and, as the trilogy will finally show [the third play was never completed], the utmost evil that could be done to him'.[28] The inspiration that enables him to transcend this evil comes from his knowledge of material truth, that is, that there is no God, no heaven, and no hell; that all men's conscious and subconscious thoughts and desires are matter, and unaccountable to any Christian or other religious law. Despite this coherent description of the tragic situation, the plays do not succeed, because Davidson saw no need to invent a new form; because he was too eager to get his 'message' preached; and because, in at least the two Mammon plays, he took his ideas out into the realm of political action. The plays may have been an attempt at allegory, but there is enough that is prophetic of twentieth-century dictatorships and atrocities, atrocities done in the name of ideologies, to force us to reject them.

Davidson's first mistake was to think that he could use Shakespearian drama and blank verse as his model:

> it is not necessary that a new drama in a new order of the Universe should deviate outwardly from the general form of all drama; nor is there any need, in England at least, to invent a new style of utterance. We have blank verse: age cannot wither it nor custom stale its infinite variety.[29]

Despite some fine blank verse and, in at least *The Triumph of Mammon*, a coherent plot and sequence of dramatic scenes, the form simply could not sustain his views. In fact, *The Theatrocrat* is more of a melodrama than a tragedy. Supposedly, the love interest and human passions of Tristram Sumner (the theatrocrat), his wife, and their respective lovers, are to provide the motives and forces of the plot, but they do not. There is a sense of suspense in the first act in saving the theatre from the barbarian onslaught of American vaudeville, but the melodramatic plot, filled with smelling salts and fortune telling, and the technical gimmicks, such as lost letters and characters hiding behind screens, reduce the play to an imitative and slightly absurd concoction of the old and the new.

The Theatrocrat is too obsessed with Davidson's materialist message. The long speeches describing his theory drown out what conflict and drama there is in the play. Nevertheless, like his testaments, the play has its own embedded self-criticism: at one point, a character behind a screen falls asleep while two others expound their theories. Davidson himself explained the limits of his message by saying the world was not ready to hear him:

> This age is too commercial, too entirely in the grip of economics: it is too immoderate in its pleasure in every kind of moral suggestion, every kind of

F

> temporary interest and ephemeral issue, to care for
> poetical drama, too abject in its haunt of dulcet
> romanticism, mystic piety and dwarfing comicality;
> and although the most tragic circumstance in the
> history of the world is at our doors — the failure of
> Christendom, namely — the mind, the imagination
> of our time is not yet healthy enough, not yet
> strong enough, not serious enough, not joyful
> enough, not passionate enough, not great enough
> for tragedy.[30]

Whether consciously or unconsciously, Davidson also
shows that the message is not ready for a stage
production, that is, that it has not found its right form
and tone. *The Theatrocrat* is a behind-the-scenes play, a
play about a play that is never in the end performed.
The Bishop of St James loses control of his Prologue,
turning it into a sermon that tries to tell the whole
'truth'. The audience not only refuses to listen, they
tear the Bishop and the stage apart. In the last scene of
Davidson's play, the broken props lie strewn all over
the stage and the Bishop lies there dying. This may be
Davidson's critique of the world around him, but it is
also, on one level, an acknowledgement that he has not
yet found the right form, the right words, and above all
the right dramatic embodiment.

Two of Davidson's early stories, 'Eagle's Shadow'
and 'The Salvation of Nature',[31] hint at his anxieties
about the political and social conditions of England
and his sometimes desperate wish that all problems be
resolved by an annihilation of society. In the case of
'The Salvation of Nature', the race begins again in a
Romantic, Edenic scene with a young man and a
young woman alone and in love. When Davidson came
to write his tragedies, particularly the *God and Mammon*
trilogy, he returned to this theme. The world is in a
decadent state, and there is no easy solution to its

problems. In fact, all solutions one might think of, such as social reform or diplomacy, Mammon classifies as the 'wriggling maggots on the fetid corpse/ Of Christendom'.[32]

Davidson said that he turned to tragedy 'in order to bring home the matter contained [in his testaments] by a closer application to life than is possible in dramatic monologues'.[33] Yet the choice of a political leader as hero, although it sends us back in time to his Renaissance and Shakespearian models, also forces him to talk of politics and advocate specific political action. The whole question of dramatic persona shifts slightly to the question of the ethos of the play. It is all very well, in the late twentieth century, to accept Mammon's making love to Guendolen when they are not married, or his love-making with Inga Volsung. Even burning down the Abbey might be seen as a radical terrorist act. But to advocate, as Mammon does, that all paupers, beggars, and criminals be led to a banquet hall, feasted, and then executed, or that prostitutes must marry and have children or face extermination, is too prophetic of later historical realities to allow us to accept it all as harmless allegory.

Davidson himself was, it seems, a staid, well-dressed, and monogamous man who never, so far as we know, acted out his subconscious fantasies. (Except on himself. Townsend reports that the poet once spent all day with an acid treatment eating through a sebaceous cyst on his head. He used no anaesthetic, and his son remembered the smell of burnt tissue permeating the house.)[34] We must also acknowledge that these plays are mere fictions; nevertheless, they expose all the contradictions in Davidson's thought and the logical, inevitable consequences of his proto-fascist ideas in a political realm.

As Davidson pointed out, Shakespeare's genius may lie in the fact that he was able to live through his

creation of Macbeth and Lear, and the great evil as
well as suffering they were capable of.[35] Yet, in each of
these plays, the tyrants find their own nemesis. As
viewers, we may be fascinated with the sheer energy
and bravado of these men, even subconsciously
delighting in the acting out of our repressed sadism, but
the plays circumscribe these characters and place them
in a larger context. We sympathize with Macbeth when
he doubts and falters. We watch, with suspense, his
journey towards inevitable defeat and his tragic
recognition or awareness at the end. In Davidson's
plays, we wait in vain for any downfall.

In form, *The Triumph of Mammon* is perhaps the most
dramatic of the later plays: the pace is faster, the
conflicts, this time personal as well as ideological, are
more understandable than in *The Theatrocrat*. The
ideological debate has appropriate images and action in
the conflict between the brothers, the attempted
castration, and finally the catafalque scene where the
two murdered bodies are displayed in front of
Mammon's people. With Mammon's own doubts and
guilty hallucinations, we think we are in the traditional,
if antiquated, world of tragedy. The plot allows for
some conflict, some ups and downs in the hero's
fortunes. We even sympathize with Mammon's
parricide, since we have lived through the father's
attempt to castrate him. But Davidson ironically inverts
our expectations and makes Mammon's tragic flaw his
humanity and the traces of Christendom and religious
sentiment left in him. All this would still fit the
traditional structure, if not the ethos, of tragedy as we
know it, but Davidson then takes two steps. First, he
has Mammon conduct a little political business with
various groups lobbying for their reforms, and here the
'closer application to life' of his theme turns into
eugenics and murder. Second, there is no catastrophe,
only Mammon's successful acquisition of kingship,
women, and power.

Mammon and His Message is more of the same with no visible doubts for the hero, only stumbling blocks that he has to overcome — by robbing the bank, torturing the abbot, machine-gunning the crowd, and burning down the abbey. The play concludes with Mammon still in power, but only by virtue of his army. All have turned against him except his women and his soldiers. As others try to combat him, our sympathies shift to the counter-rebellion, but not for long, because Davidson never develops these figures as characters.

The drama of the second play in the trilogy, as well as much of that of the first, comes from the enormity of the atrocities and the grandeur of the operatic staging Davidson devised. The trilogy is set in 1907, supposedly a political reality appropriate to the date, but placed in a mythic nordic land called Thulé, with a pre-nineteenth-century regime of kings and princesses, lords and ladies, abbots and papal legates. The mob is kept at bay with an odd mixture of swords and machine guns. In the opening scene of *The Triumph of Mammon* two ships enter the harbour with a prince on board one and a princess on the other, while (outdoing *Man and Superman*) a cavalcade of no less than two motor cars and one motorcycle arrive to meet them. In the last scene of *Mammon and His Message* the abbey burns at the back throughout the action, with significant moments, such as the fall of the belfry or the final collapse of the building, punctuating the speeches. The mob occupies the centre of the stage along with soldiers, horses, and fire engines. 'A ruddy hue from the burning abbey mingles with the electric light'[36] of Mammon's palace windows on one side of the stage and, on the other side, those of his opponent, Oswald. In an earlier scene, a tourist stands in front of the gates to the Palace museum wondering why they are closed, for he wants to see the antique instruments of torture. Cries are heard from inside, and a citizen, aware of the political situation, warns him to leave. The cries, we know, come from the abbot, who is being tortured on the rack.

Some critics have acknowledged the strength of the poetry of these late plays, arguing, as G. Wilson Knight has done, that 'Davidson's dramatic poetry becomes more and more powerful and his thought more dangerous'.[37] Certainly, Mammon's disgust and anger with the world around him inspire strong, highly rhetorical passages, such as his last speech to his soldiers in *Mammon and His Message*:

> By God you understand the modern world,
> A sink and overflow of decadence
> With slimy rags and greasy fragments stopped: —
> I mean that old fatigued philosophemes,
> Deflowered religions, gelded poetries,
> Frequent the markets, haunt the minds of men;
> That rancid odds and ends of broken thought
> Still gag conceit and stifle fantasy
> To dupe the ambitious hunger of the age.
> By Mammon you must understand a world
> Purged of the faecal past; a clean-run world;
> A world begun again and wholly cured
> Of God and sin, the immaterial wound
> That pierces through and through, the open sore
> That *is* not, though its grisly hue of death
> Can frustrate vision, and its putrid stench
> Envenom all the spaces of the air.[38]

And it is perhaps true that the Mammon plays carried 'more of a sense of ruin and combustion and conflict of ideas' than reports from the 1918 front did to Padraic Colum,[39] or, for that matter, the front of 1944. But the plays do not simply report. The spectacle is grand, even of 'unbridled power'[40] but, with many repetitions, we are left with the impression here, as in the testaments, that we must take on the cause, follow Mammon, and overthrow the present regime. In less strident poetry, such as 'The Crystal Palace', Davidson returns more successfully to his Itinerant's critical observations, ones that do not preach.

NOTES

1. *The Testament of a Vivisector*, p. 5; *Poems*, p. 512.
2. *Theatrocrat*, p. 195.
3. *MM*, p. 161.
4. See Michael Timko, 'The Victorianism of Victorian Literature', *New Literary History*, 6 (1975), 613.
5. *Theatrocrat*, p. 49.
6. *Theatrocrat*, pp. 25–6.
7. Giles Deleuze and Félix Guattari, *Anti-Oedipus: Capitalism and Schizophrenia*, trans. Robert Harley et al., New York 1977, p. 4.
8. *The Testament of John Davidson*, p. 31; *Poems*, p. 544.
9. *Webster's New World Dictionary of the American Language*.
10. Letter to William Archer, 15 June 1901, BL; *Poems*, p. 513.
11. Letter to Archer, 'Thursday', BL; Townsend, p. 353.
12. Letter to Edmund Gosse, 1 October 1904, Yale University Library; Townsend, p. 350.
13. Eber Carle Perron, 'The Last Will and Testament as a Form of Literature', *Transactions of the Wisconsin Academy of Sciences, Arts and Letters*, 17 (1914), 685–6.
14. *The Testaments of the Twelve Patriarchs*, trans. and ed. R. H. Charles, London 1908, p. 1.
15. Ritchie Robertson, 'Science and Myth in John Davidson's *Testaments*', in *Studies in Scottish Literature*, ed. G. Ross Roy, 18 (1983), 96.
16. See *Poems*, pp. 518–19.
17. Letter to Grant Richards, 24 April 1908, PUL; *Poems*, p. 519.
18. Douglas Bush, *Mythology and the Romantic Tradition in English Poetry*, Cambridge, Mass., 1937, p. 468.
19. Bush, p. 466.
20. Bush, p. 468.
21. Letters to Richards, 24 April and 20 July 1908, PUL; *Poems*, p. 519.
22. 'On Interviewing: Prose Eclogue', *Speaker*, 12 January 1895, pp. 46–7; *MF*, pp. 238–40.
23. Letter to Richards, 11 August 1908, PUL; *Poems*, p. 519.
24. [James Elroy Flecker,] 'John Davidson: Realist. A Point of View', *Monthly Review*, 20 (1905); rpt. in *Collected Prose*, London 1920, p. 191.
25. Eliot, in Lindsay, p. xii; *Poems*, p. xxx.
26. *Poems*, p. xxxi.

27. 'The Week', *Speaker*, 23 July 1892, p. 107; rpt. in *Sentences and Paragraphs*, London 1893, pp. 100–1.
28. *MM*, p. xiii.
29. *TM*, p. 165.
30. *TM*, pp. 152–3.
31. *Pilgrimage of Strongsoul*, pp. 215–78.
32. *TM*, p. 116.
33. *Theatrocrat*, p. 17.
34. Townsend, p. 454.
35. *TM*, p. 164.
36. *MM*, p. 123.
37. *The Golden Labyrinth*, p. 312.
38. *MM*, p. 136.
39. Padraic Colum, 'The Poet of Armageddon: John Davidson', *New Republic*, 12 January 1918, p. 310.
40. Colum, p. 311.

CHAPTER 6

FLEET STREET AND OTHER POEMS:
THE FINAL ACHIEVEMENT

If Davidson tried to create legendary heroes in epic, narrative and dramatic fantasies in his testaments and tragedies, he chose a new and yet familiar voice as the dominant speaker of his last volume of poems. The at once ironic and engaged tone of the Random Itinerant watches and comments on the events of various excursions, many of which Davidson had already written about in prose articles for the newspapers. Davidson's search for dramatic 'personation' and appropriate voices in his poetry had led him through different experiments, on the one hand with prosaic, realistic figures such as the music-hall artiste, the clerk, and the journalist, and on the other hand with legendary figures such as Lancelot, Tannhäuser, or 'John Davidson'. But the voice of the observer and the chronicler of the age appears finally as Davidson's most personal yet most dramatic voice. *Fleet Street and Other Poems* has Davidson's usual diverse range, including the testamentary 'Cain', the jingoist 'Song for the Twenty-Fourth of May', 'The Lutanist''s lovesong, and Davidson's two last eclogues. But the volume as a whole is characterized by the observer who walks out into the world of contemporary fragmentation — a world of 'Railway Stations', 'Fleet Street', 'The Crystal Palace', 'The Thames Embankment', and 'Rail and Road' — to witness it, react to it, and chronicle it. We sense the experience of flux and contingency and at the same time the desire to order and recontain the experience. The volume is controlled by these two impulses to chronicle and to recontain, to document the experience of meaninglessness and yet to impose meaning on it.

'Fleet Street' opens with a twelve-line overture, the first line of which is an impressionistic fragment of a scene: 'Wisps and rags of cloud in a withered sky' (443). Then Davidson begins to box in the street as on a canvas, placing all the pieces 'at either end', 'above', 'below', and 'parallel'. Having drawn the picture, hinting at both stability and flux, he invites the reader to enter into the scene with a kind of auditory imagination. He asks for a passive openness to the impressions, moods, sights, and sounds of the space, an openness ultimately to the voice of Matter, to the memories lodged in Fleet Street's material: its bricks. Like Wells' *Time Machine*, Davidson's Matter takes us back in time, unfolding the hidden imprints of former moments: 'Johnson's heavy tread/ And rolling laughter', 'Chaucer, wroth,/ Beating the friar that traduced the state', and finally to:

> The rapture of ethereal darkness strung
> Illimitable in eternal space.
> Fleet Street was once a silence in the ether. (444)

'Fleet Street' is a poem about contingency. The street is presented as a catalogue of objects, fragments bumping up against each other: 'woodwork, metalwork,/ Brickwork, electric apparatus, drains/ And printing-presses, conduits, pavement, road'. Juxtaposed with this is a list of chemical elements, also components of Fleet Street: 'The carbon, iron, copper, silicon,/ Zinc, aluminium vapours, metalloids'. What was criticized as Davidsonese is in fact a conscious attempt to include 'the facts', chemical as well as historical. The list or catalogue of objects reinforces the separateness, the multiplicity, the fragmented nature of the world.

Objects on Fleet Street lose their meaning as they are
stacked one on top of the other. Nevertheless, in taking
Fleet Street back to its origins, Davidson finds some
meaning, some unifying source of stability:
'Imponderable tension in the dark/ Consummate
matter of eternity' (444). In terms of Davidson's cosmic
order the poem is about the fall from material unity in
ether to multiplicity in elements, and Matter becomes a
resolution of all contraries, of all the bits and pieces. It
is supreme, perfect. It is an ultimate beginning as well
as the end. It is both absence ('silence') and presence
('omnipresence').

   If the poem searches for meaning in origins, it also
searches for a centre. Earth, the planets, and the moon
are seen as 'offspring and the suburbs of the sun'.
Saturn's suns are still-born or abortive births: 'rubbish
revolving endlessly/ In agonies of impotent remorse/
About the planet it deserted' (446). And Fleet Street
momentarily becomes 'a little noisy London street'. The
poem entertains a debate between 'use' and 'art' with
Fleet Street bricks and Saturn's moons as the
contestants. The bricks are praised for their usefulness
in the greater glory of Fleet Street and the Empire.
They thus become a centre of the world with all news
and events coursing through electricity to them. Their
meaning comes in their service to the 'Mother of
Nations', in contrast to the beautiful moons of Saturn
which are only abortions shining in the sky. There is
unity in use:

> *The crude integrity of commonplace*
> *Cohesion even in the most exhausted, most*
> *Decrepit, ruinous, forgotten orb*
> *In some back alley of the Milky Way....* (448)

Davidson is at his best here, passionately argumentative
but integrating his materialist theories with the
everyday urban experience of his readers, finding such

oxymoronic images as 'some back alley of the Milky Way'. How much better, he claims, than the 'shapeless fragments that make up/ Aesthetic marvel in Saturn's girdles!' (448)

The poem is a perfect example of the forces pulling Davidson in two directions. He is aware of the fragmentation. His view of art here acknowledges this. Yet the desire to find some unity and control leads him to the imperialist position where all becomes sacrificed to the glory of the country. The poem itself is made up of fragments of language (impressionistic, prosaic, and scientific), and of form (realism, fantasy, and debate), while the longing for unity embraces them all in some imperialist fantasy.

Davidson's 'The Song of Fleet Street', which is another and prior attempt to deal with this material, follows 'Fleet Street' in the volume, and stands as a coda to the first poem. It begins, as 'Fleet Street' does, with the raw material of the street: closes and lanes, drains, people and bricks, machinery, brains, pen. This catalogue of pieces, which places parts of the body on a par with sewage drains, reduces all to unit value, units which are not integrated ('souls are split and intellects spent'). By appealing to the myth of the Empire Davidson dispels the fear of meaningless objects, of dirt, of brains, and of drains. He appeals to some compensatory illusion that London is the centre of the world, that the Empire is important, that business is busy-ness, that the movement is tidal in proportion and therefore exciting and important.

These first two poems situate the narrator in the midst of the material fragments of Fleet Street and forcibly centre them in either cosmic materialism or Imperial order. With 'The Crystal Palace' the contingency and meaninglessness of the object world and the activities within that world are predominant. Unlike 'Fleet Street', there is no direct imposition of some valued system. Instead we have a reproduction or re-enactment of the sense of some contingency with only hints at the possibility of some ultimate value. They are ironic hints in the manner that T. S. Eliot was later to use: hints by allusion or by juxtaposition. The absolute value, centre, or presence is felt only as a lack, as an absence.

Davidson first dealt with this visit to the Crystal Palace in a prose article for the *Glasgow Herald* called 'Automatic Augury and the Crystal Palace'.[1] The essay is another of his travel sketches: the narrator walks, observes, debates, and imagines. The transformation of the prose article into poetry is revealing. Compare the two openings:

> In the grounds Sir Hiram Maxim's flying machines are whirling seriously, and gyrate there all day earnestly occupied. The wandering Lama from Thibet doubtless conceives this to be a brilliant, magnificent rotatory praying machine in which the petitioner as well as the orison is spun about in space. (521)

Contraption, — that's the bizarre, proper slang,
Eclectic word, for this portentous toy,
The flying-machine, that gyrates stiffly, arms
A-kimbo, so to say, and baskets slung
From every elbow, skating in the air.
Irreverant, we; but Tartars from Thibet
May deem Sir Hiram the Grandest Lama, deem
His volatile machinery best, and most
Magnific, rotatory engine, meant
For penitence and prayer combined, whereby
Petitioner as well as orison
Are spun about in space: a solemn rite
Before the portal of that fane unique,
Victorian temple of commercialism,

Our very own eighth wonder of the world,
The Crystal Palace. (427)

The poem — like the article — begins off-centre with one exhibit in the display ground: a flying machine. The Crystal Palace itself is not identified until the sixteenth line of the poem. Davidson transforms the easy introduction of the verb phrase in the article into the abusive 'Contraption'. The language is broken up, and harsh sounds grate against each other ('eclectic', 'gyrates', 'A-kimbo', 'rotatory'). The prose passage makes the comparison between the flying machine and prayer in passing, but the poem takes this to a self-conscious level by starting with an attempt to name the object and the experience. 'Crystal Palace' becomes a poem about language, how to name and to talk about this new fragmented experience. The object is appropriately named with its 'proper slang', its own, its rightful name: debased language for a debased world. The word 'contraption' points to the object's function in our world, that is, a gimmick, a device, a trick, a got-up machine to manipulate. With its 'arms/ A-kimbo' and 'baskets slung/ From every elbow' it becomes an animate thing broken into pieces, made into a machine. Once 'portentous' is introduced, we conclude that pleasure has taken the place of religion, where money's vacuum land has made idolators of its consumers. A child's voice sums it up: this 'temple of commercialism' becomes a toy-contraption-machine, 'Our very own eighth wonder of the world'. Here the ironic Itinerant is able to reduce imperial Britain's superiority and centrality to child-play, and the colonies seem to know and see more than the 'Mother of Nations'. The Tartars of Thibet have introduced the possibility of another language. Juxtaposed with the language of machinery and of deceit is the language of prayer in which objects and places are sacred, and actions are rites. The juxtaposition of the two leaves us with the sense of the meaningless activity of used people, who are victims and dupes of commercialism:

> thus, passive, all,
> Like savages bewitched, submit at last
> To be the dupes of pleasure, sadly gay —
> Victims, and not companions, of delight. (429)

Throughout the poem the speaker is a guide. At times he offers the voice of the fairground hawker, inviting you to witness and to buy. At other times the voice hints at all the emptiness and the horrors that surround him. He will allow the voice of tourists to break through as they 'goad themselves/ In sheer despair *to think it rather fine*' (emphasis added).

Davidson's means of both reproducing the fragments and alluding to the absences are similar to those used later by T. S. Eliot in *The Waste Land*.[2] The speaker cannot accept what he sees, but he senses it and reproduces it in his poem. Like Eliot after him and James Thomson before him, Davidson imposes a Dantesque atmosphere on the modern urban scene:

> Some scores of thousands searching up and down
> The north nave and the south nave hungrily
> For space to sit and rest to eat and drink:
> Or captives in a labyrinth, or herds
> Imprisoned in a vast arena; here
> A moment clustered; there entangled; now
> In reaches sped and now in whirlpools spun
> With noises like the wind and like the sea,
> But silent vocally: they hate to speak:
> Crowd; Mob; a blur of faces featureless,
> Of forms inane; a stranded shoal of folk. (430)

To emphasize the fragmentary experience Davidson employs complete breaks in the line of thought or sequence of events. To hint at what is missing he

juxtaposes the antique and the modern ('Hygeia' and
'Grilled Soles'), high art (Michelangelo's Moses,
Cellini's Perseus, or Verrachio's Coleone) and the
meaningless flow of the uncomprehending mass of
people:

> Before the buffets, metal tables packed
> As closely as mosaic, with *peopled chairs*
> *Cementing them*, where damsels in and out
> Attend with food, like disembodied things
> That traverse rock as easily as air. ...
>
> (429; emphasis added)

The crowd is reduced to a 'swish and tread/ And
murmur, like a seaboard's mingled sound', or 'eddies
swirl and swing'. At one point it is a smudge on a
canvas: 'A deluge smudges out the landscape'. Lastly,
Davidson does not end this poem with any solution or
climax. The narrator misses the holiday fireworks and
leaves the reader with the same sense of meaningless
activity that the poem has explored throughout:

> This way out —
> Past Linacre and Chatham, the second Charles,
> Venus and Victory — and Sir William Jones
> In placid contemplation of a State! —
> Down the long corridor to the district train. (433)

These two poems, 'Fleet Street' and 'Crystal Palace',
and the two that follow in the volume, 'Liverpool
Street Station' and 'London Bridge', were singled out
from Davidson's work by Virginia Woolf in a 1917
review:

> To our mind these are the best of his poems. They
> are original without being prophetic, they show his
> curious power of describing the quality of matter,
> and they are full of observation and of sympathy
> with the sufferings of man. The Bank Holiday

scene at the Crystal Palace is a first-rate piece of
description.[3]

She quotes from 'Crystal Palace':

> Courageous folk beneath
> The brows of Michael Angelo's Moses dance
> A cakewalk in the dim Renascence Court.
> Three people in the silent Reading-room
> Regard us darkly as we enter: three
> Come in with us, stare vacantly about,
> Look from the window and withdraw at once.
> A drama; a balloon; a Beauty Show: —
> People have seen them doubtless; but none of those
> Deluded myriads walking up and down
> The north nave and the south nave anxiously —
> And aimlessly, so silent and so sad.

Fleet Street and Other Poems is Davidson's most successful
volume of poems. Despite complaints of other critics
that he had chosen ugly subjects and the sounds of
cacophony,[4] he is able to combine here a personal
voice, a subject matter, and appropriate metre to
convey sincerely and passionately his relationship with
the phenomenal and contemporary world of bricks, of
crowds, of commerce and technology.

The Itinerant's ironic voice is dominant throughout
the volume. His excursions take him also out into the
country in 'Rail and Road' and 'The Wasp', and to
Bournemouth Beach in 'Two Dogs'. The conversational
voice stops at various seemingly insignificant moments
to expound and to elaborate. The poet must explore all
the varieties and possibilities available. As the world
falls apart, the poet's mind finds unity and meaning in
the least, seemingly insignificant events and details. His
visceral experience of the world around him includes
the sympathetic projection into a wasp, a snowflake,
and two dogs, as well as the bricks of Fleet Street. The
ironic tone is abandoned momentarily in some poems to

present an alternative way of dealing with the urban experience. One formulation is familiar to Davidson from the nineties: the impressionist sketch. He had used it in such poems as 'London', in parts of *Fleet-Street Eclogues*, in 'Apple Trees', and elsewhere. In *Fleet Street and Other Poems*, 'The Thames Embankment' is a *tour de force* transforming the 'dingy urban images' of the river at low tide into a moment of light-filled beauty:

As gray and dank as dust and ashes slaked
With wash of urban tides the morning lowered;
But over Chelsea Bridge the sagging sky
Had colour in it — blots of faintest bronze,
The stains of daybreak. Westward slabs of light
From vapour disentangled, sparsely glazed
The panelled firmament; but vapour held
The morning captive in the smoky east.
At lowest ebb the tide on either bank
Laid bare the fat mud of the Thames, all pinched
And scalloped thick with dwarfish surges. Cranes,
Derricks and chimney-stalks of the Surrey-side,
Inverted shadows, in the motionless,
Dull, leaden mirror of the channel hung:

. . . .

       Slowly the sun
Undid the homespun swathing of the clouds,
And splashed his image on the northern shore —
A thing extravagantly beautiful:
The glistening, close-grained canvas of the mud
Like hammered copper shone, and all about
The burning centre of the mirror'd orb's
Illimitable depth of silver fire
Harmonious beams, the overtones of light,
Suffused the emboss'd, metallic river bank.
Woven of rainbows a dewdrop can dissolve
And packed with power a simple lens can wield,
The perfect, only source of beauty, light

Reforms uncouthest shapelessness and turns
Decoloured refuse into ornament;
The leafless trees that lined the vacant street
Had all their stems picked out in golden scales,
Their branches carved in ebony; and shed
Around them by the sanction of the morn
In lieu of leaves each wore an aureole. (179–80)

Scientific facts about moisture, light, and cloud formation are woven into this Turneresque[5] or impressionist poem. The lexicon of painting, metalwork, photography, and above all pottery is built up to salvage the stains and blots, the cranes and derricks, and the dull mud of the Thames floor. What the eye perceives is the art of composition, the ordering effects of natural phenomena, of the sun and air, cumulus and vapour. Scientific facts are raised to the order of art in such terms as 'magic mechanism' and 'the ancient potter's wheel, the earth' (181). Matter creates and the alert eye perceives.

In a poem such as 'Snow', Davidson takes as his subject a scientific fact of matter and then moves into a passionate account of the nature of this snowflake. Like Lawrence's carbon, the snowflake arouses Davidson's poetic fervour as he works out his theme in a complex structure and controlled metre. The scientific fact is that the snowflake's essential structure is constructed at angles of 36°. Although it dissolves in the sun, it passes through a series of transformations, shrinking all the time, yet maintaining its essential structure. The result is a beautiful display of metamorphosis and, for Davidson, of individual will and determinism, self-fulfilment and the power of the life force. The Evangelical flavour of his testaments is replaced by a catechetical question and answer: 'Who affirms that crystals are alive?/ I affirm it, let who will deny'. The tight control of the form mirrors the absolute control of the snowflake's essential form. With each new section of the poem — there are five — the poem undergoes a dissolution and reintegration of form, as the subject undergoes its own transformations. Here may be a new poetry of facts.

Graham Hough has said of the poetry of the 1890s that there were 'an immense number of explorations, many false starts and blind alleys, and not a few personal tragedies, all directed to finding some sort of accommodation between art and a bougeois industrial society'.[6] Davidson's struggle with form was a fitful search for a poetry that could somehow speak of the experience of the modern world. His achievement in 'Thirty Bob a Week', in a few lyrics, and in *Fleet Street and Other Poems* takes his work beyond the category of 'false starts and blind alleys' and into the realm of major poetry. His poems are some of the first attempts at making the modern world possible for art. Even his system of scientific materialism, although it looks back to pre-twentieth-century cosmological world views, also looks forward to the kind of private symbolic worlds which characterized the work of the great moderns, and perhaps, in his attempt to shift the locus of value and authority from man and his institutions to forces outside man, he looks forward to the post-moderns of our time (of whom, of course Friedrich Nietzsche would be one of the first).

NOTES

1. *GH*, 18 March 1905, p. 9.
2. See Turnbull, p. xxxii.
3. Woolf, p. 390.
4. See, among others, R. A. Scott-James, 'The Last Testament', *Daily News* (London, 15 June 1909, p. 4: 'There is a sort of irritated energy in his writing, a reckless carelessness as to form alternating with what seems to be a deliberate and perverse cacophony, as if the author were so obsessed with the sense of the ugliness of life

that to be in keeping with it his verses, too, must be made ugly'. See also 'The Lounger', *Putnam's Magazine* (New York), 7 (1909), 246–9.

5. See Davidson on Turner, *TM*, pp. 158–62, and Townsend, pp. 235–40.

6. *The Last Romantics*, London 1949, p. xix.

CHAPTER 7

REPUTATION

Granger's 1909 *Index to Poetry and Recitations* shows that six of Davidson's poems had already reached the anthologies by the time of his death.[1] One of these, 'The boat is chafing at our long delay', along with 'The Runnable Stag', even made it to the 1939 edition of the *Oxford Book of English Verse*, edited by Arthur Quiller-Couch.[2] All this might have pleased a good minor poet, but we can be sure it was not enough for Davidson. His ambition was to revolutionize poetry and the world: 'It is a new poetry I begin, a new cosmogony, a new habitation for the imagination of men'.[3] He wanted, in short, to be not only the antennae of his race, but a new evolutionary step in the progress of man and Matter towards total self-consciousness. His reputation might never satisfy these ambitions, but it has, since his minor vogue in the mid-1890s, enjoyed occasional flourishes, culminating in at least one critic's claim in 1983 that Davidson might be 'arguably the greatest Scottish poet between Burns and MacDiarmid'.[4]

One of the early flourishes took place before his death among a number of young ardent admirers. His iconoclasm and his vociferous critique of contemporary society and Christian ideology were able to break down many barriers that stood in the way of a new generation of writers, and many of them, some less well known than others, expressed their gratitude. J. M. Stuart-Young paid tribute to Davidson's 'fantastic prose and haunting poetry' in a dedicatory letter in his first volume of poems.[5] James Elroy Flecker, the author of

Hassan (1922), ranked Davidson with Nietzsche and Ibsen as a great modern realist, 'the greatest poet of his age' even if, as he admitted later, 'it was not a glorious age'.[6] Although we do not have any explicit confirmation from D. H. Lawrence himself, Helen Corke wrote in her memoirs that he had given her Davidson to read, probably his 1904 *Selected Poems*.[7] As I have already pointed out, Davidson's work might well have inspired Lawrence's own 'carbon theme', his abandonment of the usual ego, and his emphasis on the unconscious, the primitive, and the vital in man.

In the twenties and thirties, as the survivors of the naughty nineties grew into their memoir-writing years, Davidson's name inevitably found its way into the lists of Bodley Head, John Lane, and Rhymers' Club poets, and especially into the shorter lists of those tragic ones who died young. (Davidson was, in fact, almost fifty-two when he died.) It could be argued that the most important of these memoirs, W. B. Yeats's 'The Tragic Generation', did more to harm Davidson's reputation than any other comments before or since, whether the remarks came in part from a resentment over an early anonymous review of *The Countess Kathleen*, presumed by Yeats's father to be by Davidson — although we have no proof that it was — which said, 'there are no lines which go straight home and linger in the memory',[8] or whether they stem from a genuine difference in personality and in aesthetic sensibility, they dismiss Davidson as a blatant failure, culminating with the haunting statement: 'And now no verse of his clings to my memory'.[9]

But another point of view has been kept alive. As early as 1916, Hayim Fineman wrote a respectable study, *John Davidson: A Study of the Relation of His Ideas to His Poetry*, arguing that his independent mind, informing his work with grandeur and intensity, made him more than a minor figure.[10] This book won itself two remarkable reviews, one by T. S. Eliot in the *Egoist* as part of his 'Reflections on Contemporary Poetry' and one, unsigned, in the *TLS* by Virginia Woolf. Eliot was guarded in his praises, but Woolf was surprised that so interesting a poet was so little remembered. She praised Davidson as an energetic, passionate, and sincere poet and lauded the introduction of new subject matter into his poetry. Unlike Dante or Milton, she said, his proselytizing spirit marred much of his work, 'yet there are few modern poets who need to be reduced to their proper stature by the august shades of Milton and Dante'.[12] And finally, 'He is always an interesting poet and a far better spokesman for his time than others more mellifluous'.[13]

Other early critics would claim that Davidson stood above the poets of his time. Holbrook Jackson (1922) claimed 'the eighteen-nineties had no more remarkable mind and no more distinctive poet than John Davidson',[14] while Max Beerbohm, a friend of Davidson's, wrote in 1948 that Davidson 'had what I think the other poets [of the nineties] had not: genius (and a very robust genius)'.[15]

The kind of devotion shown at the turn of the century by A. Kerr Bruce, who 'had by lectures to Literary Societies made Davidson's work almost as familiar to the Clyde and the West Coast as the work of Burns himself',[16] may not have surfaced again, but two selected editions of Davidson's poems were put out in 1959 and 1961. R. D. MacLeod's *Poems and Ballads by John Davidson* praised Davidson as a poet of some distinction. His choice of poems reflected a more conservative appreciation of Davidson's rural and urban lyrics, which have 'much of the simplicity of the best, being free from the sophisticated allusiveness of the later generation'.[17] But it was just this later generation that was represented in Maurice Lindsay's *A Selection of His Poems*.[18] T. S. Eliot's Preface to this volume concedes that he finds Davidson's blank verse hard going and his philosophy uncongenial, but 'in everything that Davidson wrote I recognise a real man, to be treated not only with respect but with homage'.[19] He focuses on 'Thirty Bob a Week' and how that poem discovered a new idiom and a new poetic diction for the 'dingy urban images' of his time.[20] This idiom and those images do find their way into Eliot's poety, but so do such techniques as the ironic juctapostion of classic art and contemporary culture, and the Dantesque visions of the city. As Turnbull says, Davidson's later work is far closer to Eliot's style than the earlier 'Thirty Bob a Week'.[21]

Unlike Eliot, Hugh MacDiarmid was drawn to Davidson's ideas, once again to his iconoclasm and to his great ambition as a poet. In his 'John Davidson: Influences and Influence' in Lindsay's edition, MacDiarmid claims that between the sixteenth-century Makars and a few contemporaries and with the exception of Burns, Fergusson, and some Latin and Gaelic poets, Davidson 'is the only Scottish poet to whom I owe anything at all, or to whom I would be pleased to admit my debt. Davidson stood out head and shoulders above all Scottish poets of his own time. He alone had anything to say that is, or should be, of interest to any adult mind'.[22] He was encouraged by Davidson's choice of subject matter, the scientific material and the urban experience. He also praised Davidson's inventive use of poetic drama and poetic diction.

These modern voices have established Davidson at least as one of those minor figures who have influenced the great. In the second half of the twentieth century, the major work on Davidson has been done in scholarly theses in Scotland, England, and North America. J. B. Townsend, working with the large collection of manuscripts now in the Princeton University Library, wrote what has become the standard critical biography, first as a thesis in 1953, and later published as *John Davidson: Poet of Armageddon* in 1961. He describes Davidson as a poet 'endowed with a small natural gift for lyric expression', but a lack of artistic discipline prevented him from becoming a master.[23] He also argues, as did many others, that the later Davidson retreated into a world of private nightmare, abandoning his gifts in his testaments and tragedies. Alexander Currie[24] and Eric Northey have done some of the basic groundwork for any biography of the early life of Davidson, a weak area of Townsend's book, while Turnbull's edition of the collected poems in 1973 stands as a landmark in Davidson studies. As one critic has said, the edition has banished any illusions that Davidson was a poet of small output: 'The bulk counts. ... Even a casual dip into the collected poems... provides some idea of Davidson's protean qualities, of his formidable reach (if not always grasp), of his large and restless aspiration and his dogged will'.[25] Turnbull's own introduction is one of the most informative commentaries on Davidson's work, and is only a precis of his lengthy unpublished dissertation on the poet's work.[26] Both he and Eric Northey show a better grounding in the political, social, and philosophical context of Davidson's work than do the North American critics.

Despite the efforts of a few critics and poets, Davidson has still not made it out of the category of minor poets or interesting failures. His poetry is formidable in bulk and in kind. Its technical imperfections and its difficult subject matter have prevented it from being adopted as part of the canon of English studies. Still, he is recognized as one of the first poets who successfully brought the urban world into poetry, paving the way for the great modernists who followed.

Some historians of Scottish literature place Davidson beyond the Scottish pale, one claiming he was as much a Scottish poet as Conrad was a Polish novelist.[27] Another wrote that his publications showed 'little trace of their author's extraction'.[28] But others have laid claim to him, saying that 'the decisive influences were Scottish, and *un*literary; the map of his mind was determined by his Scottish environment, inheritance, and principles, by his cultural and social roots in his native community; and by the pressure of Calvinism'.[29] MacDiarmid argued in 1926 that Davidson's *Bruce* 'ought to be revived' since it was 'our best historical play'.[30]

What direction will Davidson studies take from here? Ritchie Robertson is one of the few to make claims for the success of Davidson's testaments, *The Testament of John Davidson* being 'his greatest poem, and a striking literary achievement by any standards', and Turnbull claims that the incorporation of scientific discoveries and 'the development of a highly distinctive blank verse' give to Davidson's later poetry 'something approaching major status'.[31] I have argued that his later poems in *Fleet Street and Other Poems* are the truly modern works, while all his later work, including the plays, might be seen, through our post-modern eyes, as an attempt to do away with the static subject and the fixed forms of the bourgeois world. That interpretation will always need the qualification that Davidson himself often falls back into the governing ethos and aesthetic solutions of the later nineteenth century, be it heroism, imperialism, or traditional blank verse, but the attempt is there and so are a number of real successes.

NOTES

1. Chicago 1909.
2. Oxford 1939, p. 1040.

3. *TM*, p. 167.
4. Tom Hubbard, 'John Davidson's Glasgow', *Scottish Review*, November 1983, p. 13.
5. J. M. Stuart-Young, *Out of Hours: Poems, Lyrics and Sonnets*, London 1909, p. v.
6. James Elroy Flecker, 'John Davidson', in *Collected Prose*, London 1920, p. 207. See also 'John Davidson: Realist. A Point of View', *Monthly Review*, 20 (1905), 36–49; rpt. in *Collected Prose*, pp. 189–205.
7. Helen Corke, *D. H. Lawrence: The Croydon Years*, Anotin 1963, p. 5.
8. Anon., 'A Minor', *Daily Chronicle*, 1 September 1892, p. 3.
9. 'Tragic Generation', *Autobiographies*, London 1955, p. 315.
10. Philadelphia 1916, p. 4.
11. T. S. Eliot, *Egoist*, October 1917, pp. 133–4; Woolf, p. 390.
12. Woolf, p. 390.
13. Woolf, p. 390.
14. *The Eighteen-Nineties: A Review of Arts and Ideas at the Close of the Nineteenth Century*, London 1922, p. 177.
15. Max Beerbohm, 'Looking Backward', *Observer*, 3 October 1948, p. 3.
16. Quoted in MacLeod, p. 30.
17. MacLeod, p. 5.
18. London 1961.
19. Eliot, in Lindsay, p. xii.
20. Eliot, in Lindsay, p. xii.
21. *Poems*, p. xxxii.
22. MacDiarmid, in Lindsay, p. 47.
23. Townsend, p. 492.
24. Alexander Montieth Currie, 'A Biographical and Critical Study of John Davidson', B.Litt., Oxford 1953.
25. Herdman, p. 80.
26. A. R. Turnbull, 'A Critical Edition of the Poems of John Davidson', Ph.D., Aberdeen 1973.
27. H. Harvey Wood, *Scottish Literature*, London 1952, p. 7.
28. J. H. Millar, *A Literary History of Scotland*, London 1903, p. 664–5.
29. Kurt Wittig, *The Scottish Tradition in Literature*, Edinburgh 1958, p. 243.
30. [MacDiarmid, Hugh] C. M. Grieve, *Contemporary Scottish Studies: First Series*, London 1926, p. 233.
31. Robertson, p. 87; *Poems*, p. xxx.

SELECT BIBLIOGRAPHY

Works by John Davidson in Chronological Order

Diabolus Amans: A Dramatic Poem. Glasgow 1885; New York 1976.

The North Wall. Glasgow 1885; London 1893; New York 1976.

Bruce: A Drama in Five Acts. Glasgow and London 1886; London 1893.

Smith: A Tragedy. Glasgow 1888.

Plays. Greenock 1889. (Includes *An Unhistorical Pastoral, A Romantic Farce, Scaramouch in Naxos.*) Reissued as *Scaramouch in Naxos: A Pantomime; and Other Plays.* London 1890, 1893.

Perfervid: The Career of Ninian Jamieson. London 1890.

The Great Men and A Practical Novelist. London 1891.

In a Music-Hall and Other Poems. London 1891.

Persian Letters. By Charles Louis, Baron de Montesquieu, Trans. and intro. John Davidson. 2 vols. London 1892. Reissued as *Persian and Chinese Letters.* Washington and London 1901.

Laura Ruthven's Widowhood. With Charles J. Wills. 3 vols. London 1892.

Sentences and Paragraphs. London 1893.

Fleet Street Eclogues. London 1893.

A Random Itinerary. London and Boston 1894.

Ballads and Songs. London and Boston 1894.

Baptist Lake. London 1894.

Plays... Being An Unhistorical Pastoral; A Romantic Farce; Bruce, a Chronicle Play; Smith, a Tragic Farce; and Scaramouch in Naxos, a Pantomime. London and Chicago 1894.

A Full and True Account of the Wonderful Mission of Earl Lavender, which Lasted One Night and One Day: with a history of the pursuit of Earl Lavender and Lord Brumm by Mrs. Scamler and Maud Emblem. London 1895.

A Second Series of Fleet Street Eclogues. London and New York 1896.

Miss Armstrong's and Other Circumstances. London 1896.

For the Crown: A Romantic Play, in Four Acts. Done into English by John Davidson from François Coppée, 'Pour la couronne'. London 1896.

The Pilgrimage of Strongsoul and Other Stories. London 1896.

New Ballads. London and New York 1897.

Godfrida: A Play in Four Acts. New York and London 1898.

The Last Ballad and Other Poems. London and New York 1899.

Self's the Man: A Tragi-Comedy. London 1901.

Testaments. No. I. The Testament of a Vivisector. London 1901.

Testaments. No. II. The Testament of a Man Forbid. London 1901.
Testaments. No. III. The Testament of an Empire-Builder. London 1902.
A Rosary. London 1903.
The Knight of the Maypole: A Comedy in Four Acts. London 1903.
The Testament of a Prime Minister. London 1904.
A Queen's Romance: A Version of Victor Hugo's 'Ruy Blas'. London 1904.
The Theatrocrat: A Tragic Play of Church and Stage. London 1905.
Holiday and Other Poems. London 1906.
God and Mammon. A Trilogy. The Triumph of Mammon. London 1907.
God and Mammon. A Trilogy. Mammon and His Message. London 1908.
The Testament of John Davidson. London 1908.
Fleet Street and Other Poems. London and New York 1909.
Sonnets. By William Shakespeare. Intro. John Davidson. Vol. XXXVIII of *The Complete Works of William Shakespeare.* Ed. Sidney Lee. New York 1909, pp. ix–xxi.
The Poems of John Davidson. Ed. Andrew Turnbull. 2 vols. Edinburgh and London 1973.

Selections

Selected Poems. London and New York 1904.
The Man Forbid and Other Essays. Intro. Edward J. O'Brien. Boston 1910.
Poems by John Davidson. Ed. R. M. Wenley. New York 1924.
John Davidson. Ed. Edward Thompson. London 1925.
Poems and Ballads by John Davidson. Ed. R. D. MacLeod. London 1959.
John Davidson: A Selection of His Poems. Ed. Maurice Lindsay. London 1961.
Three Poets of the Rhymers' Club: Ernest Dowson, Lionel Johnson, John Davidson. Ed. Derek Stanford. Cheadle Hulme, Cheadle 1974.

Criticism

For a list of works about Davidson see my 'John Davidson: An Annotated Bibliography of Writings about Him', *English Literature in Transition,* 20 (1977), 112–74.

Bridgwater, Patrick. *Nietzsche in Anglosaxony: A Study of Nietzsche's Impact on English and American Literature.* Leicester and New York 1972.

Bush, Douglas. *Mythology and the Romantic Tradition in English Poetry.* New York 1963.

Chapple, J. A. V. *Documentary and Imaginative Literature, 1880–1920.* London 1970.

Colum, Padraic. 'The Poet of Armageddon: John Davidson'. *New Republic,* 13 (1918), 310–12.

Currie, Alexander Monteith. 'A Biographical and Critical Study of John Davidson'. B.Litt., Oxford 1953.

Eliot, T. S. Preface. In *John Davidson: A Selection of His Poems*. Ed. Maurice Lindsay. London 1961, pp. [xi–xii].

Faas, Egbert. *Poesie als Psychogramm: Die dramatisch-monologische Versdichtung im viktorianischen Zeitalter*. München 1974.

Ferguson, Fergus, ed. 'Biographical Sketch'. In *Sermons by the Late Rev. Alexander Davidson*. Edinburgh 1893.

Fineman, Hayim. *John Davidson: A Study of the Relation of His Ideas to His Poetry*. Philadelphia 1916.

Herdman, John. 'John Davidson in Full'. *Akros*, 9 (1974), 79–82.

Hubbard, Tom. 'Irony and Enthusiasm: The Fiction of John Davidson'. *Scottish Literary Journal*, 11 (1894), 71–82.

Jones, Howard Mumford. 'A Minor Prometheus'. *Freeman* (New York), 6 (1922), 153.

Knight, G. Wilson. *The Golden Labyrinth: A Study of British Drama*. London 1962.

Lester, John A., Jr. *John Davidson: A Grub Street Bibliography*. Charlottesville, Va. 1958.

Lester, John A., Jr. 'Friedrich Nietzsche and John Davidson: A Study in Influence'. *Journal of the History of Ideas*, 18 (1957), 411–29.

Lester, John A., Jr. 'Prose-Poetry Transmutation in the Poetry of John Davidson'. *Modern Philology*, 56 (1958), 38–44.

Lindsay, Maurice, intro. *John Davidson: A Selection of His Poems*. London 1961.

[MacDiarmid, Hugh] C. M. Grieve. *Contemporary Scottish Studies. First Series*. London 1926.

[MacDiarmid, Hugh] 'John Davidson: Influences and Influence'. In *John Davidson: A Selection of His Poems*, ed. Lindsay, q.v., pp. 47–54.

MacLeod, R. D., intro. *Poems and Ballads by John Davidson*. London 1959. First published as *John Davidson: A Study in Personality*, Glasgow 1957.

Northey, E. 'The Poetry of John Davidson (1857–1900) in Its Social, Political and Philosophical Contexts'. Ph.D., Newcastle-on-Tyne 1976

O'Connor, Mary, 'Did Bernard Shaw Kill John Davidson? The Tragi-Comedy of a Commissioned Play'. *Shaw Review*, 21 (1978), 108–23.

Peterson, Carroll V. *John Davidson*. New York 1972.

Robertson, Ritchie. 'Science and Myth in John Davidson's *Testaments*'. *Studies in Scottish Literature*, 18 (1983), 85–109.

Stoddart, Jane T. 'An interview with Mr. John Davidson'. *Bookman* (New York), 1 (1895), 85–7.

Stonehill, C. A., and H. W. *Bibliographies of Modern Authors* (Second Series). London 1925.

Thatcher, David S. *Nietzsche in England, 1890–1914: The Growth of a Reputation*. Toronto 1970.

Thouless, Priscilla. *Modern Poetic Drama*. Oxford 1934.

Townsend, J. Benjamin. *John Davidson: Poet of Armageddon*. New Haven 1961.

Turnbull, Andrew R. 'A Critical Edition of the Poems of John Davidson'. Ph.D., Aberdeen 1973.

Turnbull, Andrew R., ed. and intro. *The Poems of John Davidson*. 2 vols. Edinburgh and London 1973.

Wilson, Jean. 'The "Nineties" Movement in Poetry: Myth or Reality?' *Yearbook of English Studies*, 1 (1971), 160–74.

Woolf, Virginia. 'John Davidson'. *Times Literary Supplement*, 16 August 1917, p. 390.

Yeats, W. B. *Autobiographies*. London 1955.

Yeats, W. B. 'The Rhymers' Club'. In his *Letters to the New Island*. 1934; Cambridge, Mass. 1970.